AVENUES OF PLEASURE

ROBIN DERMOND HORSPOOL

Salutations to
25
in loving gratitude
for all it has given me,
cradle of my true self.

British Library Cataloguing in Publication Data.
A catalogue record for this book is available from the British Library.

ISBN 1 902645 35 9

Published by

Highgate of Beverley

Highgate Publications (Beverley) Limited
4 Newbegin, Beverley, HU17 8EG. Telephone (01482) 886017

Printed by Highgate Print Limited
4 Newbegin, Beverley, HU17 8EG. Telephone (01482) 886017

ACKNOWLEDGEMENTS

Though this is a personal account it has been helped to crystalise through past talks with my late parents and brother in particular. I acknowledge their memory with loving gratitude. I wish to thank my sister, Marion Wrightson, M.B.E., whose experience of the war years has been of great benefit as has her patient answering of my many questions.

My grateful thanks also go to Diana Boston of The Manor, Hemingford Grey, for her permission to quote from her mother-in-law's published autobiography, *Memory In A House,* the story of Lucy M. Boston's passion for The Manor which became the 'Green Knowe' of her famous children's books; to The Society of Authors as the literary representative of the estate of A. E. Housman for permission to quote from *A Shropshire Lad;* to William Nicholson for permission to use a line from his play, *Shadowlands,* a line he repeats often as he, like me, believes it to be true; Chris Lee of Victoria Avenue who was invaluable as an insight into the importance and efficiency of The Avenues and Pearson Park Residents' Association; to my cheery friend Ray Williams, who was equally invaluable as an enthusiastic accomplice in the Avenues with measuring tape, sheets of statistics and merry measurer's whistle, sharing in laughter at my developed lack of metric understanding; the helpful staff at Hull City Archives; Dr. John Markham and Barry Sage of Highgate of Beverley for their good-humoured tolerance.

And to my wife Rose I must not forget my apologies for those car journeys with me at the wheel. Some have been punctuated by sudden but necessary requests to jot down a bit of dictation on the back of a petrol receipt for fear that a thought or phrase is forgotten.

The poetry, unless otherwise accredited, is by the author as are the line drawings and cover design.

CONTENTS

Preface v
Introduction vi
I The House Next Door 1
II Domum Dulce Domum. 11
III A House of One's Own 19
IV A Room of One's Own 27
Interlude 44
V Personalities 46
VI Land of Lost Content. 62
Interlude. 70
VII Look Forward to Yesterday 71
Envoi 79
Further Reading 81

ILLUSTRATIONS

Princess Bank Estate, 1875 6
Pearson Park entrance en fête, c.1900 8
Tramlines and wires negotiate a Princes Avenue fountain . . 10
Maurice and Madeleine – an excellent match 12
25 Park Avenue 18
Drawn from memory: Maurice's study 21
The student nurse 28
Ground floor plan of 25. 30
First floor plan of 25 30
Drawn from memory: The parlour complete with insulating
   tape lattice and later plastic crystal chandelier . . . 35
A tree for all seasons: the silver birch's assuring presence . . 37
A good blaze warms The Shack 40
The grandparents' dog, Simon, joins the family pose, 1953 . . 46
Robin, Marion, Peter and Simon 49
Peter in characteristic attitude with a screwdriver . . . 56
A picture of content 59
Golden Rod from 25 63
25 undergoes surgery 73
A future for the past? 7 Salisbury Street moulders away . . 74
The past with a future. 7 Salisbury Street reborn . . . 74
These fallen idols will rise again 76

PREFACE

At the time when most young boys are deciding they want to be pop stars or footballers, a clutch of down-to-earth maiden aunts annually indulged my increasingly fanciful love of candles. They humoured me by contriving a game to be played during the family's collective Christmas party at their Yorkshire home. It consisted of a parade ground of candles marshalled into ranks on an oblong tea tray. The winner was the fire-raiser who managed to ignite, with one match only, the greatest number.

The game, potent in its simplicity, was called 'Robin's Delight'. Charades, the highpoint of the festive proceedings, could hardly hold a light to my fascination with the assorted colours and sizes of smooth and barley-sugar-twist candles, sentinel like some pagan wax henge initiating worship of their glowing sun-like solstices.

Even at that early age, this idolatry of candle power evoked in me a tangible sense of the past which seemed neither alien nor remote and in which I felt comfortable indulging my whims and fancies; I had not been born with an imagination for nothing. The past has always had a mystery I find lacking in the modern world. It must be because it is removed from everyday experience and needs discovery, which in turn needs imagination.

Like some novice time-traveller on a training day, I created in my bedroom old-fashioned room settings and their contents to complement my enduring addiction to candles, more than happy to live part of my life in a world of my own making in which I was master of myself. It has never been a penance to go about duties of the present couched in the knowledge of the past; it is like being on loan to the real world until willing re-absorption into an illusion which happens to be compatible. Could this be due, I wonder, to a strain of dissatisfaction somewhere deep down which needs a certain kind of selective fulfilment, some kind of shock-absorber for life's frustrations and disappointments?

It is strange to reflect that what were childhood fantasies and explorations, now help to pay the mortgage, the coal bill and sustain the flow of good red wine. As Art Lecturer in Period Decoration and Style at a local College of Further and Higher Education, my early love affair with history and its re-creation in decorative terms has been of enormous benefit. I teach what I am, both the theory and practice, and can find no blade thin enough to separate my creative crafts from myself.

Candles, too, are firmly ensconced in this double existence. Rose and I inhabit a converted Wesleyan chapel in a Wolds village, the large main living space of which is the setting for 96 candles not intended for decoration alone, particularly during Christmas and power cuts.

And Rose joins me in discouraging neither.

Robin Dermond Horspool
December, 2002

INTRODUCTION

The future is nothing, but the past is myself, my own history, the seed of my present thoughts, the mould of my present disposition.

Robert Louis Stevenson
Essays of the Road

The house opened onto a big lawn surrounded by the rushy moat, another surprise. I had not known of its existence. Beyond the moat were meadows and a small orchard. It was all instantly lovable and possessed at first sight . . . As I went into it first it was the atmosphere that took me by the throat and filled me with a welcoming and headlong excitement . . . I was myself again and the spell of the house strong on me. Since one supposes stones and mortar cannot of themselves exert influence, I am always left wondering what it can be to which I respond personally and inescapably.

Lucy. M. Boston
Memory in a House

We read to know we are not alone.

William Nicholson
Shadowlands

I

THE HOUSE NEXT DOOR

There was a boy went forth every day
And the first object he looked upon, that object he became,
And that object became part of him . . .
For many years or stretching cycles of years.

Walt Whitman
Leaves of Grass.

The Great British Public has cultivated a corporate fascination with where it lives, what it lives in and how it lives in it.

Even though the heavens may open, damp but spirited hoards insist on tramping ducal drives and heritage matting, trusting that element of surprise, delight or revulsion which greets the unseen owners' displays of trees and flowers, furnishings and fabrics, pictures and plate.

This voyeuristic public has fashioned an art form out of looking in on itself in order to compare and contrast; to be stimulated one way or another during that singular static shuffle particularly suited to contemplative appraisal: the monastic ruin, the feudal pile, the country seat and countless swerving acres of outstanding natural beauty. We are looking at anything from some historic bastion almost submerged by its weight of national identity to the understated domesticity of Mr. Straw's semi-detached in Worksop. Visitor Centres cater for the distilled commodity presented as instant access; gift shops and plant sales ensure that you carry a little of your appraisal back to your own environment.

The media, too, fosters and promotes this appraisal with teams of camera-conscious enthusiasts ripping up other people's turf and assaulting their walls and ceilings with unforeseen colours and textures. Cameras invade spaces and their contents with the precision of keyhole surgery; erudite minds team up to root around in cellars and attics in order to expose the properties' mysteries and pedigree. The media has presented us with The 1900 House, The 1940 House and The Edwardian Country House assiduously re-created and endured by participants willing to obey the restrictions of the time; 18, Folgate Street, London, is living history as an alternative way to modern life by shunning technology and science in favour of drama, romance and inconvenience. Living history centred round the human, its habitat and possessions has never had a more public nor global following. But history is brought alive only by human involvement – history *is* human involvement on all levels, with the humans themselves as much a source of study as their environments.

I confess to being a member of The Great British Public. A devoted member, in fact, habitually intrigued with how successive generations have interacted with and contributed to creating an enhanced survival. This need to contribute is as inevitable as our passage through the galleries of our lives in the hope of enlightenment and self-awareness.

I am as well tuned to coping with life's heatwaves and cloudbursts as I am to the effect on me of seeing any sign bearing the legend HOUSE OPEN TO VISITORS or GARDENS OPEN TODAY.

It was at the invitation of this latter that I found myself, a little while back, making for the Pearson Park neighbourhood of Kingston upon Hull. My visit to the 19th-century residential development was the result of learning that certain households in the Avenues opposite the Park bravely opened their gardens for a couple of weekends in the year irrespective of weather or potential mud baths. My visit was not planned to coincide with a reliably wet English summer afternoon – sunshades or umbrellas are one and the same to the gardening fraternity and mine could double as either though my wellingtons were more specific. Despite the downpour, I was amazed by the enthusiasm and even dry humour of the visitors. I was heartened, too, by their obvious appreciation of the loving care sown by garden owners with as much profusion as the flowers, features, shrubs and trees. They enhanced the dignity and scale of an area which, in the modern city, still retained its muffled aura of scented, leaf-clustered retreat. It composed the verdant courts and quadrangles of some seemingly Arcadian university whose motto, borrowed from Virgil, might well be: *FORTUNATUS ET ILLE DEOS QUI NOVIT AGRESTIS.*★

Having graduated the courts by degrees I began studying the back garden at number 27 Park Avenue, a fun-fair of sheds and summer houses, pergolas and pavilions, winding paths through artefacts and knick-knacks, wind chimes, figurines and a great deal of mosaic concocted from bright fragments of tiles and crockery. As if it were needed on such an afternoon as this, a waterfall at the end of the garden tried to out-splash nature as well as the overflowing fern-fringed grotto intended to contain it.

As I looked back at the house I noticed through the thinning crowds someone with an identical umbrella to mine staring intently through the fence on my right. He sometimes moved in order to see over it, sometimes bent down to peer through convenient gaps. He seemed to have no interest in the garden he was in nor its other visitors; in fact, he gave me the impression he would like to break through the fence and disappear from view.

I naturally looked over the fence to see what could be of such riveting interest. I felt I must be blind or daft for I could see nothing that seemed to warrant it. In fact, it was easy to see why this garden, which must belong to number 25, was not on the open list as there didn't seem to be one. That is to say there was a space, but it was featureless, like an economical mask, though the house was occupied. Rough unattended grass created an undulating green depression – a desert of expectancy devoid of features, surrounded by inquisitive poplars, chestnuts and sycamores kept at bay by defiant hedges.

★ Fortunate is he who knows the country gods.

But still the man stared. And as I stared at him, I sensed something familiar about him and automatically began moving closer. He was about my height and build and in the slim infancy of middle age – my contemporary. He had a pleasing, rather classic face with a nose that might have suggested a not altogether English ancestry. He wore his brown hair longish over his ears and as I approached him he turned to look at me with dark friendly eyes. It was then that I recognised him.

'It's Robin, isn't it?' I said, holding out my hand. 'I thought it must be you. Have you lost something?' He clasped my hand with a warm firm grip despite the rain and smiled wryly.

'In a way I have,' he half laughed, pitching his medium-light voice to combat the water gurgling down a nearby drain. 'But it was many years ago. I used to live there. I wanted to see what it looked like.'

'There's not much to see,' I said helpfully. 'Is it as you remember?'

He shook his head. 'It's changed much over the years – the house has too by the look of it. I don't know if I have. Fancy seeing you here.'

'I'm very fond of The Avenues,' I replied, 'even in bad weather. I've known them all my life.'

'Same with me,' he said, shaking residual water off his umbrella. 'Being able to get into this garden gives me the chance of seeing into mine. I still consider it mine, you know. It must seem odd to you.'

'On the contrary,' I assured him. 'I understand completely.'

'And you see that window up there?' he continued, pointing upstairs at the side of the wing projecting at right angles to the house's main body fronting Park Avenue. 'That used to be my room. At one time my entire world was concentrated behind that glass. It was my window on the world. It was enough for me.'

'Part of that old world still remains glazed there I'll be bound,' I said as if I knew what he meant. 'I expect it always will. It's strange, isn't it, how worlds expand the older you get but time to explore them gets shorter.'

'I couldn't have phrased it better,' he said, wishing he had said it first. 'It's uncanny that you know what I mean. You've often said things I'm thinking for as long as I've known you.'

'And I've always known that you like exploring your worlds. Where better to begin than your old world? I would be interested to explore it with you – be your navigator. Exploration is much more fun with a companion. We've known each other a life time and we understand one another, I think.'

He looked at me quizzically as if he had not expected a sympathetic reception. But over the years he must have come to realise that we had much in common, for a certain relief tempered his earnest face.

We arranged to meet again in dryer circumstances and for him to let me into the secrets of his self-awareness and the obvious significance in his life of the house next door. I was intrigued to know what he had meant in answer to my question when he said that in a way he had lost something.

As our meetings increased from then on, I began to comprehend his reason for drawing my attention to a handful of lines by the American poet Walt Whitman.

'I could have been that boy he wrote about,' he told me. 'As I went forth every day, I became the first object I looked upon. That first object was my life at 25 and, of course, it became part of me. It was my identity – my security. Hence my sense of loss when it was superseded by a newer life. You will understand me when I tell you that I think I have been looking for that lost security throughout all my new lives.'

'And why you feel safer with the past than the future?'

'The past is the only security we have – it has happened – it is known about. The future could give way at any second, like the untried ice on an anonymous lake.'

I smiled appreciatively. 'I must say,' I ventured, 'you do have a way of expressing yourself – it can be quite poetic at times. Have you swallowed a slice of Whitman pie?'

He said that he liked the discipline of poetry and the way so much can be conveyed with the minimum of words, if they are the right ones. It's a case of getting at the *truth* of what is felt and meant.

Feeling and meaning were obviously high priorities of this erstwhile and somewhat eccentric companion, so, knowing of his addiction to history, I decided to do some research on both our behalfs. It was necessary, before dealing with ways of life and personalities in the Avenues, to place them in some sort of historical context, particularly as their layout had been conceived a generation before Hull's promotion to city status by the Royal Charter of 1897.

Back in 1860, 20,000 people in festive mood had spent 27th August not only watching and cheering a celebratory procession but also witnessing the signing of the deed of conveyance of 27 acres of land in north-west Hull intended as a new park for the people. The People's Park was the gift to his home town of Zachariah Charles Pearson, a 39-year-old merchant with a passion for the sea which led him into owning a fleet of steamers. A self-made businessman too, his gift of land celebrated his year of office as Mayor. He retained a further ten acres of perimeter land on which to build houses served by a broad carriage drive round the park. This encircling carriage way enabled the ten acres to become the site of substantial Italianate dwellings. This had a two-fold purpose: not only did he wish to provide an attractive and healthy rural space easily accessible to all citizens, but also to encourage the professional classes to reside within a mile or two of their places of work and offices in the town centre. These provisions were much in line with that popular breed of bewhiskered Victorian philanthropist jostling for plinth-hold in public estimation.

But unlike them, there was hardly time for his name to be lauded with Hull's newest amenity than bankruptcy dislodged him. He resigned as Mayor during his second term of office in October,1862, his creditors, friends and public at large aghast at the gamble which had caused it: his purchase of a fleet of ships on credit with which to run arms through southern ports blockaded by President Abraham Lincoln as part of the American Civil War. Most of Pearson's ships were either taken or burned, representing a hole in his exchequer of £85,000.

But pride, along with tenacity, had always been one of Pearson's qualities, so, instead of running away to hide in disgrace, he and his family left their roomy residence on Beverley Road, accepted help and support from friends, finally settling at 2, Elm Villas, (now 63), in the park he gave his name to. Trading as United States Commercial Agent, Shipbroker and Coal Exporter, he remained a park resident for the rest of his life, dying on 29th October, 1891, a year after his wife.

It was only a matter of time before the land immediately to the west of Pearson Park was developed, and there is no doubt that Zachariah Pearson would have cast an interested eye on what was happening beyond his threshold of trees and lawns, boating lake and bandstand.

In 1874, 230 acres of open land dotted with a few farms was bought by David Parkinson Garbutt, 24 years Pearson's junior, a Hull-born businessman, ship-builder, property developer and eventual target for creditors. Intending to continue the residential theme of this rural retreat, he called his purchase the Westbourne Park Estate, Westbourne signifying its position west of the Hull/Cottingham boundary or 'bourne' which ran down beside the western edge of Pearson Park. Garbutt also sensed with his entrepreneur's nose that 'Westbourne' had an aristocratic ring about it which might act as bait to clients of discernment.

The bourne was a rough agricultural track with a ditch either side and popular as a country walk. It was known variously as Mucky Peg Lane, Newland Tofts Lane and Sculcoates Occupation Road. Under Garbutt it was soon straightened, resurfaced and re-christened Princess Bank Avenue. With Zachariah Pearson as guest of honour, the 'fine thoroughfare' was opened on a sunny Easter Monday in 1875, alive with bunting, music and animated crowds, many of whom were from out of town. The Police Band near the marquee at the park entrance accompanied a good trade in soft drinks and refreshments. *The Hull and Lincolnshire Times* enthusiastically reported that at one o'clock the barriers at either ends were removed so that the Most Gracious Queen's loyal subjects and the whole world could pass through. The presence of Sir Charles Adderley, President of the Board of Trade, added to the significance of the moment, as did the playing of the National Anthem, followed by cheers for Mr. Garbutt and his family.

The report of 3rd April also mentioned the laying, some time earlier, of the grand avenue's foundation stone. This was on the corner of the southern-most avenue of four which Garbutt laid down at the same time at right angles to Princess Bank Avenue, or Princes Avenue as it eventually became known.

From south to north, Marlborough Avenue was named after Marlborough

House, at that time Garbutt's ponderous block of a residence on Anlaby Road, guarded by two stone lions. Next came Westbourne and then Park, an obvious choice. The farthest avenue was Victoria, a tactful allusion to the monarch nearly 40 years on the throne. All four ran about three quarters of a mile from east to west before petering out into open countryside and sunsets behind the eventual site of the Hull and Barnsley Railway.

It was a prestigious area in which to sell building plots, as land agents' prospectuses were keen to point out. Advertised as Princess Bank Estate, they enumerated its advantages as a healthful residential suburb convenient for gentlemen engaged in business in the town. They drew attention to the excellent modern drainage down the centres of the roads and at the sides, to which plots could easily be connected. They praised its situation for being kept smoke-free by the prevailing westerly winds; they praised its footpaths and wide grass verges planted with trees affording pleasant shade and a park-like appearance, as well as the advantages of being next to The Park itself.

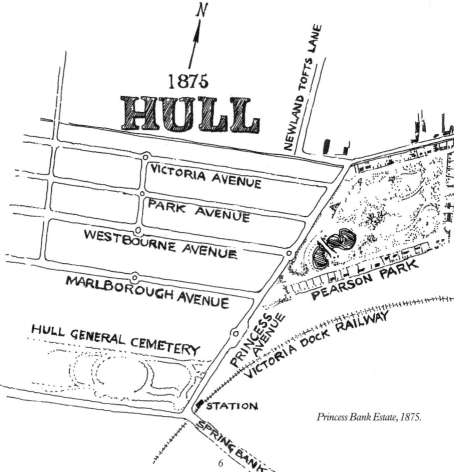

Princess Bank Estate, 1875.

6

By 1880 the first plots were being filled – the majority of interest being in Westbourne Avenue, which was 20 foot wider than the others. Substantial brick terraces were going up along the south side and also on the west side of Princes Avenue; on Salisbury Street, running north to south between Park and Westbourne, a group of extremely stylish dwellings designed by George Gilbert Scott, Jnr. elevated their Dutch gables and swags of stucco fruit and flowers amongst the geometry of squared sash windows. With piecemeal speculative building now underway, the development promised a refreshing variety of styles and scales, making for architectural interest and individuality.

This individuality had been one of the component parts of the Princess Bank Development from the start by its emulation of the new boulevards of Paris then being driven through the old city by Baron Haussmann. They became the fashionable byword for generous thoroughfares redolent of moneyed taste and secure style.

One of the choicest features of this taste and style in Garbutt's scheme was the happy introduction of what were called 'circuses' at strategic points over the acres. There were two on Princes Avenue and four in the Avenues themselves. They were circular, in the form of cast iron fountains, to integrate with the ornamental railings, gas standards and thriving foliage contributing to the area's Continental character. Marlborough and Victoria contained differing and undemonstrative examples, later to be removed. But the other four asserted their full-blown authority with a blatancy that must have encouraged many a passing cyclist to slow his pace and quicken his pulse. A quartet of naked mermaids with conches jammed to their lips made a clean breast of their mission as guardians of the large ground-level basin. Their canopy was a smaller basin watched over by herons who themselves snuggled under an even smaller basin fed by a decorative spout pointing straight into the air about level with the surrounding rooftops. Water spurted, splashed, trickled and dripped, not least from the conches of the alluring maidens, shooting at an angle of 45 degrees into their extensive round reservoir thoughtfully fenced off to a height of nearly six feet to deter the young at heart.

As the crinoline of the 1860s and the bustle of the '70s and '80s gave way to the leg-of-mutton sleeve and wasp waist of the '90s, houses and villas began gradually to flesh out the bones of Garbutt's structure. There had been no way of telling whether the area would become popular, though expectations were high, considering that, in the 30 years since Pearson Park was opened, Hull's population had doubled to 200,000. By the early 1890s, 38 households were resident in The Park, 30 in Princes Avenue, 21 in Marlborough, 52 in Westbourne, 26 in Park and 16 in Victoria. The Avenues counted among their residents bankers, shipbuilders, wine, coal and timber merchants, a tea merchant and a bank clerk. Some of the properties contained facilities for stabling horses and small domestic vehicles; these coach houses were arranged to have access from lanes or 'ten foots' running parallel to the Avenues to divide the back-to-back gardens from each other. The only gardens not so serviced were those on the south side of Park Avenue backing on to the north side of Westbourne.

Though the size of the houses varied, at least one live-in domestic servant would be catered for, with a bedroom in the attic or a small room at the back of the house; a good middle-class address needed to be ordered and kept clean, with the Master of the House stepping smartly out to his place of business each day with his creases pressed and collars starched; the Mistress stayed at home, received visitors, paid calls and saw that a comfortable, well-run household was worthy of being on show at any time. So the tone which was to identify the area for the next 70 years was set.

By the early 1900s, a number of streets parallel with the Avenues had been laid out on land to the south reaching down to the corner of Princes Avenue and Spring Bank. Known colloquially as 'The Dukeries', they took their aristocratic names from five imposing English estates: Blenheim, Belvoir, Clumber, Thoresby and Welbeck. They were intersected by Chatsworth and Hardwick Streets. Commercial properties were also integrating in this developing area, with Princes Avenue, or Princess Avenue as it was still known, becoming a fashionable shopping parade for the butcher, the baker and candlestick maker.

Where Princes Avenue, Spring Bank and Spring Bank West met, the Hull to Withernsea and Hornsea railway line provided a small country station called Botanic Gardens. The name commemorated a 49-acre stretch of land which had opened in 1880 as a Botanical Garden. Its limited success lasted only a few years when its site was used to establish Hymers College, a first class school for boys. The Jacobean-style building designed by John Bilson had the advantage of an already mature parkland setting in keeping with the nature of the neighbourhood.

Pearson Park entrance en fête, *c.1900.*

8

This seemed a convenient juncture at which to acquaint Robin with my findings. He became as immersed in them as I was, but had a particular desire to single out his own avenue, about which he seemed to feel almost proprietorial. This led me further to share and discuss my findings.

At 60-feet-wide, Park Avenue was 20 less than Westbourne. Neither of us could explain why we thought the Avenues were not of equal width. What took our fancy even more was the coincidence that at the time Hull received its city status, the house he was eventually to live in was being created. The plans, which are dated 18th April, 1898, are for a set of 12 semi-detached houses on the south side of Park Avenue at the Pearson Park end. The drawings bear the stamp of Gelder and Kitchen, the prestigious firm of Hull architects. They were currently responsible for a certain civic identity in improvements to the new city: slum clearance, wide thoroughfares and dignified buildings. These were happy manoeuvres as not only was Alfred Gelder an architect but also a councillor; and, like his buildings, Gelder's life was structured to carry weight at many levels, embarking as he did in 1898 on his first year as Mayor. But instead of providing land for buildings like Pearson before him, he provided buildings for land. He also created something of a mayoral record by being elected for another four consecutive years.

So the terrace of 12 houses on the drawing board can be seen as representing a crucial crossroads in Hull's development – a symbolism put into concrete form by the builder J. E. Wray.

With five bedrooms and gardens front and rear, the houses were soon ready to put on the market at under £800. Charles Charter and Co., one of Hull's leading estate agents, lists many Avenues' properties in his Homefinder publication, Westbourne Avenue commanding prices in excess of £1,000. Charter's Property List would describe the type of dwelling Gelder and Wray had provided as a well-appointed semi-detached villa with entrance hall, two reception rooms (one with bay and one with French casement), kitchen, glazed veranda, scullery (copper and sink, hot and cold water) and five bedrooms (one with bay), bathroom and lavatory (h&c), two W.C.s and gardens front and rear. Though like the Avenues themselves, the early houses were lit by gas, by 1910 Charter's Property List begins to instance electric light, electric bells, all modern conveniences; whereas ten years previously houses were advertised as having a coach house or stabling facilities, phrases like 'ample space for motor house' or 'concreted motor house with double folding doors' appear. You could call in at Charter's office in Bond Street and rent a desirable modern five-bedroom residence in Victoria Avenue for £35 *per annum*. Whether you rented or purchased, you could be certain you had made a wise move for your neighbour at 103 would be your agent.

In the years following the Great War, during which a house in Victoria Avenue received a bomb from a Zeppelin, the growing rings on the Avenues' trees were outdistanced by the massed humanity cut down in the trenches of Flanders and the Somme. The Park had taken on a homely, leisured ambience and the Avenues, too, acquired a more furnished look with the increase in building and improvement of public transport services. The popularity of cycling in such a flat city had accelerated since the 1890s; then came the electric tram, which had reached Spring Bank corner at the southern end of Princes Avenue by 1900. The system was powered by overhead cables suspended from tall ornamental cast-iron supports, the vehicles grinding and clanking along tramlines let into the roadway but careful to swerve round the mammary fountains.

From the terminus in the city centre, travel over any distance cost one penny, journeys coloured by the livery of crimson lake and white, with *City of Hull Tramways* picked out in gold along the outside. For those passengers who were disabled ex-servicemen, relaxing with their free passes in the varnished wooden interior, it was a livery worthy of their traumas and sacrifices on the fields of battle.

By 1936, improvements in the system were already in hand as a new trolley bus service was inaugurated which would do away with the need for tramlines (always a curse cyclists were railing against), but not the overhead cables. One of the earliest passengers was a 31-year-old clerk at Midland Bank, Beverley Road. He alighted, all six foot of him, and strode purposefully up Park Avenue clutching details of a house for sale. His other hand swung a brief case on which was stamped his name, Maurice Arthur Rupert Horspool.

II

DOMUM DULCE DOMUM

The house is old, the trees are bare
And moonless bends the misty dome.
But what on earth is half so dear –
So longed for as the hearth of home?

Emily Brontë

'He was my father,' said Robin. 'He had been married for five years and had a three year-old daughter, Marion. Now that a second child was on its way, his house at 80, Silverdale Road, where Marion was born seemed to have halved in size. Something with four or five bedrooms would be just the thing; 25, Park Avenue sounded ideal on paper but at £450 might be a bit steep, particularly as it needed exterior and interior attention. But one of the perks of a career in the bank was the financial assistance available for deserving causes. With a methodical and level-headed approach typical of Maurice, he and the bank made the necessary arrangements, and before long, some bright black woodwork was included in a substantial amount of painting, decorating, distempering and whiting of ceilings by Mr. E. Grantham of Walker Street for the grand total of £13.13.6d. After further work by bricklayer and plasterer Mr. R. Grantham of Hill Street, the expectant family moved-in in time for the birth, the following January, of a son, Peter.'

Marion and Peter had been born to parents who had first met whilst still at school. Maurice was the son of Robert Horspool, Art Master at Bridlington School; and his wife Madeleine was the daughter of Peter Louis Dermond, proprietor of Powolny's Restaurant in Hull's King Edward Street, an establishment of formidable excellence and reputation. Coincidence would have it that their premises had also come from the drawing boards of Gelder and Kitchen a few years later than 25.

Maurice's career as a banker had started on 3rd May, 1922, at the age of 17 when his duties at the King Street branch in Bridlington consisted mostly of filling up inkwells and being given threepence by the manager from time to time with the directive to get his hair cut. His transfer to Driffield in February, 1923, treated him to the plain-speaking and often ribald humour of the direct Wolds folk who did not balk at speaking their minds, even over the counter. Notorious for not using two words where one would do, these farmers and their wives were just as likely to call a spade a spade and a debit a lot worse, with copious references to the excretory habits of animals. His seven mind-broadening years among them contrasted markedly with his next move to the hushed respectability of Silver Street in Hull, where he at last felt his career promised to show some direction. By the time Peter was born, he and his brief case had transferred to Beverley Road, an easy bicycle ride from Park Avenue in suit, mac, trilby and cycle clips.

But Maurice's working life had broader prospects than merely the next column of figures. An intellectual with a dry sense of humour, his passion for the written word, and drama in particular, encouraged him to roll alongside his banking duties a prolific career as a journalist, author, playwright and lecturer. His broadcasts, too, for the North Region and Hull's own radio station, 6KH, became as familiar to him as wads of banknotes, the successful outcome of his humanitarian approach through continued involvement in public work. His belief, when pressed, that he thought he had a pleasing personality which inspired confidence was an understatement typical of his humility and gentlemanly charm.

The long-standing bond of love between Maurice and Madeleine brought a sense of unity and dependability to their new house. Madeleine was, however, not new to the area, for as a young girl she had lived at 122, Park Avenue. Unlike her husband who was from a thrifty, scholastic Bridlington family, she had been brought up in the more affluent and socialising theatricality of Powolny's in the city centre and her later Newland Park home in the country near Cottingham. Both locations enhanced her larger-than-life parents and their susceptibility to being temperamental; they had, between them, the natural ability to make life's one, act plays into three-act dramas. Inherently

modest and shy like her husband, Madeleine had inherited the best qualities from her parents: loyalty, common sense and an infectious sense of humour and fun, as well as a love of the creative arts, particularly music. As a married team she and Maurice formed the cornerstone on which the Park Avenue family were to build and rely.

Yet this could have gone so horribly wrong, for, with the birth of Peter in the front bedroom at 25, Madeleine contracted puerperal fever

Maurice and Madeleine
– an excellent match.

despite (and probably because of) the attentions of Nurse Jackson. Here was a malady which had damned many an early marriage and childbirth in the past - a serious type of blood poisoning generally from the hands of midwife or doctor. Had its treatment and cure with sulphonamides not become common practice after 1934, Maurice would have had to face the future double-strengthened by his customary philosophical approach. Fortunately, though it was a slow process, Madeleine responded to treatment but was unable to cope with the new baby and household duties. Through a banking acquaintance, Maurice heard of a recently retired elderly nanny who was unable to settle after a lifetime's caring for other people's children. In mid-February, 1937, Miss Henrietta Morley joined the family for perhaps a few months. She ended up staying nearly 20 years.

Three more autumns turned the leaves of the limes and chestnuts outside the bedroom windows as life returned to some semblance of normality. The house continued to have its chimney stacks and roof tiles repaired by Mr. King the joiner and its gutters and downpipes cleared by Mr. Hanby the plumber, who charged 1s 4d for wiping as good a joint as any to be found in Hull.

The European joints of civilisation were in dire need of sound wiping as 1939 approached its autumn, if increasing news coverage of Nazi Germany was a watertight indication. Then, on the morning of Sunday, 3rd September whilst Marion tricycled round the sunny garden celebrating her sixth birthday, the Prime Minister's clipped and cold cadences informed Britain that she was at war with Germany. Marion, remarkably mature and self-possessed for her age, accepted explanations to her questions as matter-of-factly as if she were doing her schoolwork.

Each day she trotted across Park Avenue in her white blouse, brown box-pleat tunic and beret edged in yellow to Brentwood House at No. 6. For the last year she had been attending this small private prep school for boys and girls run by Miss Colley, Miss Martyn and a grey fluffy dog called Jim. It was one of several in the Avenues, Froebel House in Marlborough being the most enduring. Teaching and learning continued despite a threatening atmosphere which lasted throughout that initial period known as the 'phoney war' before German bombers appeared over Hull and air attacks began punctuating daily and nightly routines. At Brentwood House, the kitchen ceiling was shored up with pit props in case of disaster and an air raid shelter constructed in the back garden where lessons were continued, if necessary fortified by a pack-up of biscuits and chocolate to nibble over a particularly sticky bit of long division.

At 25, she helped her father fill hollow concrete blocks with sand as he used them to construct an air raid shelter in the back scullery with an interior space large enough for five wooden bunks and five people including Nanny, all of whom were at present having to fit in the cupboard under the stairs during raids. But now they were becoming more frequent and aggressive, so permanent protection afforded by concrete blocks beneath a nine inch concrete roof and cemented to a concrete floor hastily took up most of the scullery.

A sufferer from varicose veins and bronchitis which exempted him from active service, Maurice had rejoined the Special Constabulary, having first become an officer during an earlier national crisis – the General Strike of 1926. For a time after that he had not pursued its demands but was now back in the rank of Inspector. He would finally leave after the war as Divisional Commandant.

One of the dangers of living in Hull was its importance as Britain's third largest port and therefore a powerful target for disruption and demoralisation. Residents in the Avenues responded, like all other residents, to the rallying call of posters asking for any spare domestic cooking utensils and metalware to be donated to the cause of manufacturing munitions and weapons. Miles of ornamental railing and indulgent scrollwork, so carefully integrated by the Victorians, was set upon by hacksaws and tossed into the back of lorries. The fountains' mermaids, for the first time in their lives, found themselves exposed to the full glare and vulnerability of the harsh modern world. Mischievous incendiary bombs left scorch marks on roads and pavements round them, which were accompanied by assorted fragments of shrapnel and shell cases, providing Marion with the most comprehensive collection of size, weight and deformity in her class. She remembers men in uniform occupying a house near the fountain; they were prone to run out of it every so often with a large gun, mounting it on a large tripod in the middle of the road and pointing it largely into space. These were believed to be part of the Royal Scots Battalion who had earlier come to defend the East Riding in case of attack. They now had billets in Hull, using properties in Westbourne and Park Avenues and Salisbury Street.

The amount of ironwork missing in Pearson Park was compensated for by the strategic placing of more guns, with, high overhead, a massive barrage balloon straining gently at its moorings fixed on the Queen's Road sector of the lawns. During one particularly ferocious storm, the balloon, struck by lightning, exploded in resounding flame. With many an 'ooh!' and 'aah!' from the windows of Brentwood House, the children watched the blazing tatters lizarding down through the veils of rain like venomous tongues steaming with rage.

Though the boating lake mirrored the unchanging cycle of seasons and changeable weather, it was the winds of change which troubled its waters as 1940 progressed. A heavier air of uncertainty and unease hung over the landscape. In the garden at 25, Marion looked up into her favourite tree, a gracious silver birch, and listened to the atmosphere as it soughed strangely through its delicate tracery, aware that the sounds were increasing in volume until, with a sudden roar, an aeroplane burst over the house roof behind her making her spin round and stare. Spread in the sky like a predatory bird it swept low enough for her to see the pilot in his cockpit in the same moment as her mother rushed out of the house in near hysteria to scoop her up as the 'plane sloped out of view over Westbourne Avenue. She recognised it as a German fighter at the same instant as registering pops of anti-aircraft fire spasmodically flowering the sky with distant puffs.

Some days later, Nanny took her into Hull to see a Messershmit which had been shot down and was on display in Queen's Gardens. Whether it was the same plane there was no way of telling, but the reality of war had suddenly been brought much closer to home; from that moment, Marion and Peter were automatically put to bed each night in the newly completed shelter.

They were awakened in the small hours of 8th May, 1941, by the undulating wail of the air raid warning siren, a prelude to such a night of destruction the likes of which Hull had yet to experience. Marion was most disgruntled at not being allowed out to see what was happening, quite unperturbed by the thundering booms and vibrating foundations. Only when they seemed to be getting nearer and stronger did she sense the controlled panic of her mother and Nanny as they nervously counted a punctuating advance of increasing bangs. Then the ground beneath the shelter shook as a deafening explosion enveloped the shattering of glass and rumble of chimney pots down tiles. Alarming as all this was, it was nothing compared with the racket made by the heavy wooden towel rail fixed to the scullery door being blown from its screws and landing with a series of ear-splitting clatters on the echoing concrete threshold of the shelter. This was too much for Marion. Having endured loud disturbances of nights' sleep hitherto with customary equanimity she now, for the first time, demanded her ear-plugs.

The sounding of the all-clear and return of daylight revealed that 25 had not been hit nor the surrounding houses. The bomb, which had obviously been the last in the stick dropped over the area, had demolished property on the corner of Westbourne and Princes Avenue. The next would have done away with 25. As Brentwood House was still in tact there was to be no legitimate absence from school that morning. Maurice had been firewatching as usual with the Special Constabulary overnight. Stationed in the centre of Hull, he had witnessed the havoc of those hours – hours which saw the heart of Hull torn out, including Powolny's Restaurant. His father-in-law had died four years previously, a merciful escape from the trauma. That was in reserve for his son, Paul, Madeleine's brother, who had been continuing the business and living in one of the Gilbert Scott houses at 7, Salisbury Street.

Alarmed at the uncertainty and danger normal life in Hull now presented, she and Maurice decided that for the time being, removal to a safer location was the logical solution. Her widowed mother had independently taken a flat in Harrogate, which made the obvious choice evacuation to Maurice's elderly parents in Bridlington. Arrangements were hastily made, Robert and his wife Marion overjoyed at the prospect of having their grandchildren and daughter-in-law with them. They made no secret of their relief, having been sick with anxiety at the sight of blazing Hull's glow in the southern sky.

Little Marion was in the middle of an art lesson when Miss Colley entered the room and told her that her father had come to take her away and that she must leave at once. This did not go down at all well as the artist wanted to finish her picture first. But she was told, gently but firmly, that Daddy couldn't wait. Methodically she rinsed her brush, and, as the scarlet paint blooded the swirling water, she left the home ground she was not to see again for a further six years.

Once Maurice's refugee family were safely deposited 30 miles up the coast, he turned his attention to his own situation - one of resounding loneliness in an empty 25, though he kept himself occupied with his creative writing and the business of living which was brightened by week-end visits by bus to Bridlington.

He teamed up with a colleague from the bank whose own family had evacuated to Carlisle, moving into his house at 53, Westbourne Avenue, where Nanny was also installed as cook and housekeeper. Number 25 was emptied, the furniture put into store, then let to Hull City Council to use as a billet for wardens, fire-watchers and as a depot for dry goods such as gas masks and blankets.

Within a year he rented a house in Bridlington for his absent family, easing the pressure of their living with his parents. Number 9, Fourth Avenue, was within walking distance of the sea and, when furnished with their own possessions from store, at least made a self-contained unit for the unknown duration of the war.

Bombing demolished 113, Princes Avenue, once home of the Victorian marine artist, Thomas Somerscales, and Malvern House in The Park, where Foster Earle had lived in a style afforded him by his family's cement business. His brother, Thomas, the sculptor, was responsible for the statues of Queen Victoria and Prince Albert visible across the lawns from his windows, blind witnesses to such destructive history in the making.

Maurice, now promoted as 2nd officer to a branch on Holderness Road, spent as much time as possible with his family, re-weaving some strands of normal married life which, however fragmentary, led Madeleine to reach Christmas of 1943 thinking she might be expecting. This was unexpected, unplanned and potentially alarming. She was 35 – considered a more risky age for childbirth then than now; Peter was almost seven and Marion ten. It would mean purchasing another pram, but as the baby was not due until the following July, there was plenty of time to make necessary arrangements. One of these, in the light of complications at Peter's birth, was to have Madeleine under scrupulous care in the maternity wing of the Avenue Hospital in Westgate, an elegant 18th century mansion in the Old Town near Bridlington Priory. She was to have the personal attention of Miss Slack, Matron and old family friend. Marion was overjoyed at the prospect of a new baby, never considering the possibility of it not being a sister. She was temporarily out of sorts with boys as Peter was proving to have a stubborn tendency not always to comply with her wishes. The new addition, she decided, was to be named Pauline and trained up to be the perfect minion.

July 6 was an auspicious day in the annals of the Avenue Hospital for it unwittingly celebrated the new baby's arrival into the world's sunshine by holding its annual Garden Party at the same time. It was, by no means, a conscious arrangement on either side – rather the contrary, for as Matron, immaculate in flowered frock, picture hat and presentation gloves, was about to have much pleasure in declaring the event open, an urgent message from the labour room caused her to flee the dais calling fervently for 'aprons, hot water, more hot water!' It is not difficult to savour a surreal image of baby being stylishly hauled into the world by the matronly model of *haute couture*, fresh from a summer garden, smelling more of dahlias than Dettol. The outcome was a boy.

He first saw the afternoon sun through a Georgian sash window. Though he was unequipped, at the time to appreciate this startling revelation, he subsequently wondered if it was in any way responsible for his natural view of the world. The blueprint of his being had already left the factory at conception, ordaining that mostly due to his father and partly to Germany's Furher, he should be born a Cancerian with all the emotional trappings its sway contains: sensitivity, vulnerability, and a sense of self-protection. With home orientation the focus of survival, the Cancerian is a romantic, his colour all shades of green, his destiny guided by the moon, his life's motto interpreted as 'passive resistance is the best form of attack'. Marion the Virgo was horrified at the curse of another brother and wanted him sent back. Peter, placid, easy-going and Aquarian, did not agree. Their brother was christened Robin at Sewerby Church. As soon as Hitler heard of him he committed suicide whilst the Russians sacked Berlin on 30th April, 1945.

With the cessation of hostilities, Maurice's paramount concern was to reinstate a family life which had been truncated so vehemently nearly six years earlier. No. 25, though thankfully a survivor of the Luftwaffe, had not escaped unscathed from the Corporation's indifference. Its abject neglect and cold squalor represented to him a period of enforced repression. The prayer now was that it would all gradually level into a less threatened and more hopeful civilisation in which his children could grow up.

In the meantime there was much to make good: forced doors, broken sash cords, smashed windows and locks, rotten woodwork, damaged tiles and gutters causing massive water infiltration and a back garden obliterated with thistles. Maurice was able to claim compensation from the War Damage Commission out of which £16 went to Stepney Contractors of Alexandra Road for the demolition of the indoor air raid shelter, and a further £23 for repairs to the kitchen and scullery. Nanny, who had remained at Westbourne Avenue throughout the war, bristled with brushes, mops and a vigour which belied her age while the furniture from the Bridlington house was returned and 25 made welcoming.

On 6 March, 1946, she waited sentry-like on the front doorstep eager for the new baby's arrival. Here was the perfect opportunity to defer that threatening doom of retirement she so dreaded. She knew Marion and Peter were too old for her now and, besides, they were to remain at boarding school in Bridlington. But the youngster could not be a more suitable age. He was a heaven-sent excuse for her to remain with the only life and family she possessed. Maurice, out of gratitude for her devoted and caring wartime service, could not find it in his heart to ask her to go, despite his wife's misgivings – misgivings which must have seemed ominously pertinent as mother and child arrived at 25: Nanny removed Robin from her arms with, '*I'll* take him now, thank you. We don't want him catching cold, do we?'

25 Park Avenue.

III
A HOUSE OF ONE'S OWN

The House: my earliest place
Of sound and sight and touch
In England's green and gardened land;
Home unquestioned, unchallenged,
Unassailed – as much
A part of me as face or hand.

Over the next few years, while 25 repossesses the family relationship as though the break had been nothing more than stopped animation, its newest resident begins to absorb his surroundings and accept the increasing familiarity with the ease of the poetical boy going forth every day. Where the stupendous lime tree stands sentinel on its verge plot before the house, an elderly Nanny appears round the pram's hood to fuss the coverings. She adjusts the pram's position in the front garden so that the morning sun, tumbling the stratas of leaves like a golden waterfall, should not engulf baby's frail craft nor dash his delicate eyes. Had baby any inkling of coherent speech he would have told Nanny not to be so blooming silly – that he loved the green-fingered warmth; that being summer-born he always would, and wanted to be sun-blasted all his days amongst the power of nature.

That reckless dependence on the security of the real world confronts him every time he returns home with Nanny from an airing until, as he outgrows his wheeled transport and accompanies her on foot with submissive hand anchored in hers, he can take stock of it. It is manifest in the house he lives in: red brick, ivy-clung, square front garden demarked by neat privet, lilac, lawn, golden rod. To the right, a passage between 25 and 27 giving access to the back garden.

The front path leads to double porch doors painted, like the rest of the woodwork, a sympathetic holly green. On the right a bay window rises through two floors giving that period of late Victorian architecture its comfortably 'arrived' look, with a single flat sash window above the porch. Once under its semi-circular glass fanlight proclaiming the house's individuality – 25 flashed in gold – the holly green front door protects but invites, with glimpses through its panels of ruby glass etched with frosted foliage, birds and scrollery.

The threshold, by the early 1950s, represented to the increasingly independent child a conscious assessment of the house's geography and interaction with family experiences and emotions. The first door in the hall on the right belonged to his father's study with front bay window; next along, the light airy sitting room with apple green woodwork and cream plaster walls. It was lit by a distinctive bay window with gabled glass roof and side lights comprised of coloured glass leaded together in fancy almost *art nouveau* patterns. French doors led to the back garden. At the hall's farthest end, beyond the staircase on the left, the old kitchen, now the dining room, retained its high mantel shelf and friendly range set between banks of deep cupboards and drawers built into each alcove. Lastly came an enclosed veranda, pantry, coalhouse and scullery-kitchen – all painted bottle green and cream and full of scrubbed pine tables and shelves. Upstairs, a great deal of landing and corridor united a small room nestling over the front porch with two good-sized bedrooms with ample windows and fireplaces. Down four steps at the back of the house, two further rooms lay over the veranda and kitchen. Bathroom and W.C. separated the two sections of the house. The staircase, lined on the wall side to waist height with a thick arabesque anaglypta, stepped up, chunkily parading turned spindles. A magnificent bulbous and fluted newel post terminated a long stretch of mahogany handrail to be long polished by swift descents of well-worn trouser seats.

Since being built, no kindly-meant 'improvements' had been perpetrated on its honest fabric – no awesome examples of easy-to-clean khaki-tiled fireplaces to replace the monumental dust-catchers so perfectly in proportion with the rooms; no labour-saving boarding up of banister rails and panelled doors; no stripping out of plaster ceiling roses nor cornices; no replacement windows at odds with their surroundings. Generous woodwork, deep skirtings and ripples of moulding all blended in architectural compliment as they were first intended. Electric light had superseded gas with carbuncular brass switches sprouting at door surrounds to every room.

As Robin grew older, some rooms began to identify themselves with particular seasons: the kitchen in summer with Nanny heaving the week's wash into the bubbling copper in the scullery, its fire beneath crackling and roaring as she sloshed through steam and suds creating a new language with ribbed wooden washboards, ribbed zinc dolly tubs, wooden dolly sticks (which looked like milking stools on broom handles), and copper poshers (what looked like colanders on more broom handles). She poshed, pushed, pulled, pummelled, dollied and thrubbed until, after miles of sopping survivors had been posted through the clanking mangle, they were pegged out exhausted on clotheslines zigzagging the garden. The dining room was for winter, its plain walls and green woodwork blushed by a neat fire behind the bars of the green and cream mottled range all ovens and trivets. Here was a hotbed for the black dumpy kettle expertly perched, with a contented song oscillating from its Pickwickian rotundity decked with a cheery feather of steam. Autumn illumined the back bedroom upstairs – a square south-facing luminescent space overlooking the garden and well-planted neighbourhood. All painted soft white, it had an intricate cast-iron fireplace on the left of a bay window lined with broad window seats inviting perpetual sun.

But it was his father's study which transcended all seasons and seemed to resound in his developing awareness of a tangible world. It was almost entirely lined with old books in hunky glass-fronted cases slabbed like sky scrapers

Drawn from memory: Maurice's study.

from floor to ceiling. It retained its original woodwork finish, painted and varnished to represent deep mahogany. How well it suited the Turkey red carpet flashed with greens, blues and ochres; the hand-tinted Gillray engravings suspended on cords from the grained picture rails like bumbling insects squarely caught in brown cobwebs. Maurice's creaking Edwardian swivel chair and kneehole desk took up a central position, an altar of *bric-à-brac* and fluted brass pillar lamp with eerie green glass shade. No surface nor corner was uncluttered beneath the white globed light fitting mountaineering its way down from the craggy encrustations of its ornate plaster anchorage.

A ponderous composition of polished black slate created, on the chimney breast, what might easily have been mistaken for the sarcophagus of some mighty mogul or potentate. It enclosed a hearth and surround of William Morris-style ceramic tiles, their medieval colourings emphasised by the gun-metal sheen of its cast-iron inset and grate. The furnishings, like much of the rest of the house, dated back 50 years or more, having been picked up cheaply at auction sales during Maurice and Madeleine's early married life. A bank clerk's salary had allowed them to purchase mostly out-dated items at knockdown prices – oriental carpets, pictures in gold frames, decorative objects – solid good quality pieces with a style and potential which would see their values in the ascendant over the next 50 years.

Maurice's study, with its close, rather musty smell of books and tobacco, was the first room to register on his young son's conscious involvement in an environment. It was through its windows he saw Nanny slip on the icy front path; saw his first fall of snowflakes; heard his first strains of Verdi and Wagner; was continually fascinated by its jumble of objects and artefacts, everyone a duster's nightmare: the plaster statuette of Scrooge with his money bags; the piercing cuckoo clock above the filing cabinet; a photogravure representation of an elegant young man lolling against some Classical ruins, his expression bearing signs of patient suffering, as well it might with nine arrows piercing parts of his anatomy.

Most personal, though, was a perfectly ordinary cigar box, grubby, lidless, torn green and red label with DEXTER'S KEY WEST COLORADO MADURO printed all over it. Inside, a congestion of oddments: small oval frame without a picture, bits of scarlet sealing wax, a gold watch on half a chain. There were also several glinting rectangular cut-glass lustres from a chandelier, faceted and pointed more wonderfully than anything to come out of King Solomon's mines. Robin had no idea then what they were but fell instinctively in love with them, mystical fragments of treasure prismed with a thousand tints and hues. He would pore over these glittering prizes for hours, holding them between finger and thumb to drink the light through their rainbow contours. He pressed them against his face – his tongue – in an attempt to become part of them. The odd one out, more beautiful than the rest, was of the merest green, as lambent as swells of sunlight through a spring leaf. He felt as if he belonged to them as much as they belonged to their box. They represented his identity with the room and all he required of life – it was enough. They were each other's secrets.

* * * * *

Life, however, required more of him, and with Nanny in the forefront of his upbringing, he graduated to Bricknell Avenue Infant School from his nursery school in Cottingham, an establishment memorable for cleaners' buckets behind screens serving as the boys' *pissoir*. He was already showing a tendency to work only at what interested him. There was very little of interest at school he decided, except art and singing; games were rough, arithmetic was hard, water was wet and so was he, always catching colds and remaining puny. Marion and Peter, on the other hand, with a ten and seven-year head start respectively, were showing strength of character in their academic lives.

Though both of average ability, they understood the value of disciplined mental application and hard work in order to equip them for a quality of life to which they aspired. In 1949, Marion became a day-girl at Newland High School in Hull in order to study for her School Certificate whilst living at home. She had hated being a boarder at Bridlington High School. On her 17th birthday in 1950 she applied to St. Bartholomew's Hospital in London, affectionately known as Barts, enabling her to fulfil her life-long ambition of becoming a nurse. A year later she began her training, Peter remaining at Bridlington School.

Just when Maurice and Madeleine could have been anticipating a lessening of parental worry, their youngest child was ripening into a troublesome fruit, not helped by a certain confusion in his perception of which authoritative female he was expected to relate to – the elderly, with dark clothes, wheezy breath and admonishing tones, or the younger and move attractive, with a musical voice, colourful clothes and a smile to drown in. Young as he was, he sensed a friction between them, an uneven see-saw on which it was difficult to find some sort of balance.

In the meantime, his environment was widening as Nanny introduced him to trolley bus rides from the end of Park Avenue into town. The last of the maroon trams had run at the end of June, 1945, having been phased out by this newer system distinctive in its blue and white livery. The vehicles became a familiar sight along Princes Avenue as the 62, its pair of antennae on top of the roof clamped onto the overhead power lines, coursed along like some humming insect. The prospect of a roadshow to break the journey was never far away as the antennae were prone to come off their moorings, at which the conductor and driver would extract a long flexible pole stored under the bus in a quiver-like pipe. They would raise it and cajole the locking device back into place – a delicate operation relying on strong arms, a steady eye and immense patience, especially in the rain. Interested bystanders relished the muttered oaths amidst bursts of sparks as power was restored to the accompaniment of appreciative applause.

Highway drama such as this was sometimes the prelude to an icecream at Victoria pier where the steam ferryboats paddled across the muddy Humber; to seeing pictures in the Art Gallery where he wondered why the kneeling marble figure of Joan of Arc with her lambs did not leap up shrieking hysterically like his sister when he tickled the soles of her bare feet. This is a ritual he continues to the present day when the attendants' backs are turned. He also remembers seeing the legacy of war in the city centre – large ragged gaps in runs of property, Powolny's opposite the 62 terminus included, but being as yet unfamiliar with its significance in the family story. Pearson Park too, was a sedate haven of peace, with ducks to feed, banana trees to see growing in a vast conservatory, glistening white statues of Queen Victoria and her Prince surveying their location with posed indifference.

It was the immediate vicinity of 25 which related most to the needs of the household as Princes Avenue seemed to hold all the commodities necessary for sustaining everyday life. Each Thursday afternoon, Madeleine would 'go along the Avenue to give my orders', as she phrased it. This entailed traversing the right hand side calling at the butcher, the grocer and the greengrocer in that sequence so that the following week's meat and boxes of provisions could be made up and delivered by a boy with a basket on his bike no later than Friday afternoon.

Mr. Abbot the butcher owned a shop whose walls were tiled throughout in delicately hand-painted ceramic murals depicting potential meats contentedly munching in pastoral meadows. Some stared appealingly at the welter of carvers and cleavers, chopping blocks, hanging carcases and blood-stained sawdust drifting the floor. Pigs' heads stared back from the window where dead rabbits and hares hung up-side-down, miniature red buckets tied underneath their chins collecting blood. It was a place easily able to persuade a young mind that the world is not as sweet as he would like to think it.

Mrs. Kirkby's grocery shop, despite post-war austerity and ration books, remained as well stocked as any self-respecting cornucopia. It was where a deft flick of the wrist round a long hooked pole could adroitly topple the most inaccessible package on the top of the top-most pile on the top-most shelf. She had an ornate silvered till whose drawer shot out to the clang of a bell when the keys were energetically pressed. The noisy internal mechanism also popped up tabs with the prices on behind a little glass window at the top like targets in a shooting range.

Podmore's the chemist was occasionally a port of call, usually if Robin was 'sickening for something'. His shop was heavy with mysterious smells and warm mahogany cases fronted with plate-glass doors full of glass-stoppered jars stuck with labels emblazoned in tantalising Latin; behind the curved glass counter, another case for brands innumerable, a stockade of little square drawers with ribbed glass knobs; and above – sheets of engraved mirrors reflecting myriad balms and tinctures. Two wooden-seated chairs guarded the counter – the sort of heavy devices designed for maximum discomfort in draughty hallways but a welcome perch whilst waiting for service or prescription. And in the window, three astronomical pear-shaped glass flagons with pointed stoppers full of coloured liquid, one a keen medicinal green.

Until he was old enough to take himself, Robin's mother sometimes took him after school to Mr. Bell's barber's shop. Its low wattage gloomed amongst fixtures and fittings dark and not dissimilar to Mr. Podmore's, the difference being the copious amounts of unswept hair fluffing the black and white check lino. Over the wash-basin before the sacrificial chair, the patchily silvered mirror registered Mr. Bell's white coat and line of hard-seated Edwardian benches lining the back wall in a cross between a station waiting room and Spartan gentlemen's club. By crossing his palm with sixpence he could electronically shave all your hair off up the back of your neck and round the sides of your head as if he was peeling an orange, whilst leaving short tufts on top resembling an abused yard brush. The older Robin got the more he objected to this assault on his person.

Miss Bayston's for fruit and vegetables was the last official call, a shady shop beneath trees near Botanic crossing where the steam trains chuntered into the trim rustic station amongst high-blown umbrellas of vapour. It was entering another dimension to dash up the slatted pedestrian footbridge spanning the tracks from Paragon Station, to become enveloped in flailing white guffaws from engines huffing beneath. The gates, too, were familiar in action, swinging across the roadway to shut it off from the tracks as trains approached, the red lanterns atop them joggling like marionettes as they jerked to a halt. Cyclists thus barred congested in shoals level with their bull's-eye glare until released to surge on with slow force into other waves of cycle power circling Hull's conducive flatness. In the gruff winter days the signal box, all glass and brass levers, glowed with green gaslight, a polished cube of minty iridescence as snug as a mug of tea.

* * * * *

With the death of King George VI in 1952 and the accession of Queen Elizabeth II, a new, more refreshing strain of domesticity permeated the household at 25, but at the expense of not a little drama. Nanny and Robin's mother had never ceased to be at loggerheads with the way he was being brought up. Nanny continued to feed him with a teaspoon whenever she could, though he was nearing eight; to swathe him in protective clothing; to instil in him the fear of physical exertion and the sin of exposing naked flesh. Whether consciously or not, she was doing all she could to sustain his dependence on her in sickness and in health, so that her services should remain indispensable in the only home she now had. Some confusion clouded his mind as he tried to work out which of his two mothers was which, particularly as the one without the family name seemed to be in charge. Madeleine became almost neutralized in a situation where her husband's loyalty to the nanny seemed to over-ride his loyalty to her. He was incapable of any knowingly unkind act, but, in not bringing about Nanny's retirement, he was being unintentionally inconsiderate to his wife. She considered that the family's debt to Nanny's loyalty had now been paid. It was at this point that the bond between Robin's parents became seriously threatened. Always prone to bouts of migraine, neuralgia and nervous irritability, Madeleine had put her sufferings to positive use as early as 1947 when 'Slippers By The Fire,' a short story she wrote and broadcast from the BBC Manchester studios, dealt with a wife's role in her husband's life being weakened by a third party. Fiercely loyal and supportive to Maurice, she felt hurt and alone, particularly as Marion was now at Barts and Peter still away at school.

She entered the back bedroom (then the nursery) one sweltering summer's day to find Nanny preparing Robin for an afternoon walk. She was horrified at the amount of clothing being applied to his slight frame, almost fighting with Nanny to strip some away.

'No *wonder* he's always catching colds!' she exclaimed as she peeled off gloves, scarves, coats, jerseys, vests. 'He needs to breathe – build up resistance!'

Perhaps there would eventually have been outright war had nature not come to the rescue. One morning, not long before the new Queen's coronation, Robin went downstairs as usual after Nanny had called him to find her in a still heap on the carpet. Mystified as he was, he had the presence of mind to go upto his parents' bedroom and wake them.

'Nanny's on the dining room floor and she can't speak.'

She was removed to Kingston General Hospital, where she remained for several months paralysed on one side and able only to stare at him when he was taken to visit her, tears staining both their faces. Her silence was unnerving; it was strange not to hear the familiar, 'Don't do that you naughty boy.' Her speech gradually returned and a certain mobility – a remarkable recovery considering she was over 80. Maurice took the opportunity of settling her in Kingston Villa Old People's Home in Pearson Park where she lived on for a few more years, popping in to see the family at 25 periodically as they did her – a frail, tough little white-haired old lady whose sole possessions had always fitted into a black tin trunk under her bed.

But she had contributed to her charge's awareness of the world around him. He would never forget those early associations with atmospheric rooms in Wilberforce House; the narrow Dickensian thoroughfares in what was left of the Old Town surrounding Holy Trinity Church; the stirring subject matter of paintings in the art gallery. These were the foundations on which the next phase of his development was built.

IV

A ROOM OF ONE'S OWN

I hear the murmur of the night wind
In the garden trees,
The steady rain amongst the frail
And autumn-bitten leaves.
I hear it harrowing the miles
With sweeping frenzy-tread,
As it drums the open tiles
That clothe the slanting roof
Above my bed.

The Avenues, like life itself, opened up their possibilities once some of the restraints on the growing lad had been placed across The Park. Robin's parents now hoped that he would develop normal boyish pursuits, of which cycling was to be encouraged. Kitted out in more lightweight clothes – Aertex shirts and cord shorts – he was sent along 'the Avenue' to buy bread with the educative purpose of bringing home the correct change from two shillings in attempts to improve his inspired misunderstanding of numeracy. He was also allowed freedom of the neighbourhood in the saddle – a neighbourhood seemingly protected from the buzz of city life and traffic. Routes were long and straight and unencumbered by vehicles either moving or static. Cathedral naves of trees created endless vistas of green-dappled light in every direction their foliage falling in November like golden confetti. The 'ten-foots' behind, with their variety of buildings, sheds and old stables, were like miniature worlds in themselves, in autumn giving speeding more spice by banks of slippery leaves releasing their musky bronze aroma as they erupted with the screech of brakes into the disturbed air.

One had to be careful not to disturb the rag-and-bone man's horse as he pulled the cart, the air resounding with a barely decipherable string of syllables approximating to, 'airr-rag-oann!' but understood by pitch and repetition as, 'any rags, bones?' The pig man, too, collected lidded buckets of potato peelings and cabbage stalks left at the pavement ends of the communal passageways between the houses.

Pedal-power brought the ice-cream vendor along on his white canopied three-wheeler and painted command to STOP ME AND BUY ONE; the knife-sharpener with his mobile carborundum wheel guaranteeing grinding spurts of sparks from axes, scissors, shears and any other cutting device produced the ring of a doorbell. On the other hand, the milkman traversed the Avenues on foot, towing his milk float by a lever handle also acting as a brake. The road-sweeper bristling with brooms, shovels and a dustbin on wheels whistled his way along the gutters and verges as did the lamp man with his ladder when he needed to tinker with the mechanism of the gas standards and clean the glass walls of the lanterns with squeaky leathers. There were those residents who remembered the days before the clockwork lighting mechanism when the lamplighter did his rounds to ignite the gas mantle with his flaming long pole. Music plunking out of barrel organs had serenaded the milkman on his horse-drawn rounds ladling milk into any proffered jug either left on the doorstep or brought to the churn. Some even remembered open meadows and orchards on the unfilled building plots, as well as carved lattice fencing running at right angles across the verges from pavement to kerb adding a quaint rusticity to the roadside language.

Young as Robin was, he appreciated that his locale had a quality about it unlike anything he had experienced elsewhere. Apart from the timbered spaces and gas illumination, he was particularly fond of a group of nostalgically romantic residences further down Park Avenue, blatantly theatrical in their towers, spires, crenellations and other castellated adornments. Most beloved were the two remaining fountains in Park and Westbourne Avenues, the others having been removed along with a good deal else in the interests of easier traffic flow or war. Like mammoth *épergnes* from some Babylonian banquet they rose in the centre of their circuses, but now

The student nurse.

28

waterless and unprotected from anyone small and lithe enough to squirm, crawl, climb and slide about the generously fronted mermaids' bumps and hollows. Painted a deep bottle green, these magnificent erections of High Victorian camp provided a veritable Venusberg of delights on their island sites, guardians of a sequestered world which had changed little since being conceived.

Changes were taking place at 25. In 1953 Peter had left Bridlington School where he had been since he was eight. He came home to live as he began his apprenticeship with the Yorkshire Electricity Board as a trainee electrical engineer. He was a happy but undemonstrative 16-year-old with a chunky look reminiscent of his Dermond grandfather. Marion, successfully completing her Barts training in 1955, returned proudly home bearing S.R.N. after her name proclaiming her a State Registered Nurse. The war had disrupted the continuity of childhood for them both and Marion, in particular, always one to give family values top priority, felt she would perhaps like to have a hand in bringing up her rather tiresome younger brother who seemed so young and immature for his age. With her ability for organisation and facial features endowed with a reliant serenity, she joined the nursing staff at the Victoria Nursing Home (later the Nuffield) opposite the fountain in Westbourne Avenue.

Whilst their parents retained their front bed-room, Marion occupied the room behind. Peter took over the back bedroom which had been the nursery, and, with Nanny no longer resident, Robin moved from the little front room over the porch to her old room next to his brother. Both rooms were reached along the corridor at the head of the stairs. It was lined floor to ceiling with built-in wooden cupboards and drawers which gave the appearance of old panelling, a feature not slow to impinge on his developing imagination.

Now he had graduated from a room ten feet by eight feet (3m by 2.44m) to a room 10 feet square, the extra space making all the difference, though it also had no fireplace. The room faced west with part of the ceiling sloping down to the window side as it followed the angle of the pitched roof. His early recognition of period style caused him to ask his mother to redecorate it in Regency stripes – silver and gold on three walls and crimson and gold on the wall opposite the window. Further, to create a sense of the antique, he applied lengths of black electrical insulating tape between the window's wooden glazing bars in what he imagined to be a good imitation of lattice.

Being now situated along the corridor in what he looked upon as his own private wing, his sudden elevation to property brought monetary benefits as well as imaginative – he received a rise in pocket money. It doubled from sixpence to one shilling, later increased to two (10p). This opened up the possibility of being able to possess genuine *objets d'art* which, if Victorian, were considered worth only a few pence at that time.

Even before he changed rooms he had been drawing oil lamps, statues, aspidistra bowls, even busts of classical composers as he became familiar with

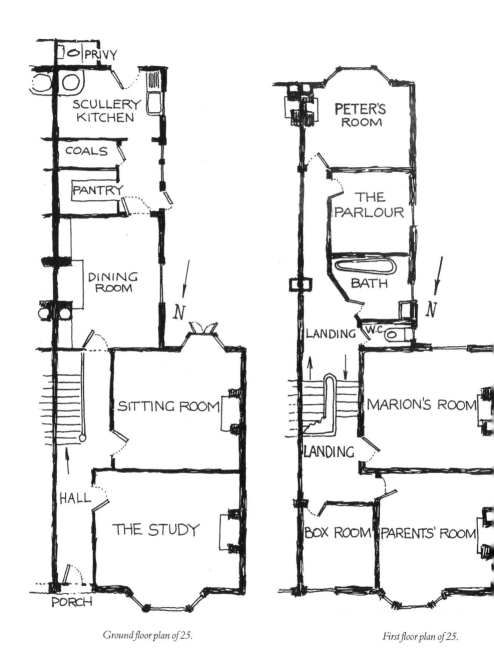

Ground floor plan of 25. *First floor plan of 25.*

their works through piano lessons and his father's gramophone. He would cut them out and stand them up, pretending they were authentic antiques. His improved finances enabled him to invest in the real thing from his local emporium where, for the first time in his life, he found he understood the value of money and how much change was due. Mr. Dring's second-hand shop became his favourite second-hand home. It lured him onto Princes Avenue between Coombes the Cobbler and Adams the Baker on the corner of Welbeck Street – a baker's shop notable for its curved corner window sheltering a towering white wedding cake of cardboard and plaster of Paris pillared up in diminishing sections on a stupendous polished silver stand. By comparison, Mr. Dring's half-lit world of curiosities and cobwebs jostled dustily together in hopeless masses which seemed a perpetual worry to him, constantly expressed by the couplet,

What a life
Without a wife!

But Robin decided that his worries could not be too great as he never attempted to tidy up and no wife ever appeared to do it for him. Besides, here could be purchased a small Staffordshire figure for sixpence, a small oil painting for nine pence and a silver stamp box for one shilling and eleven pence. His father referred to this new friend as 'The Brigand', probably wondering why his son did not spend his pocket money on sensible things like comics or bubble gum. One of his earliest purchases was a pair of unrestrained Victorian pot vases in muddy green and worn gold with pictures on the front of carthorses being led home in sunsets – bargains knocked down from half-a-crown to two-bob. 'Daylight robbery,' Maurice wisely informed his son, assessing his acquisitions as 'fine, if you like that sort of thing'. He was sad that his father and he did not see eye-to-eye on the sense of beauty and history these objects awoke in him, but then, his father's generation, having grown up with such items, was busy throwing them out, not expecting his son's generation to be getting them back again. He hoped that his father did not think he was looked upon with an equal sense of obsolescence. His family bemoaned his indivertible magnetism to what they termed 'hideous vases', uncomprehending that their main attraction to him was their abundance and affordability. But this did not prevent his father from kindly contributing some of the fifteen shillings necessary for a Country Chippendale chair and some of the ten shillings for a Georgian tripod tea table needing repair to a leg. And he had to agree with The Brigand that his son had an eye for style and a bargain.

Gradually his bedroom began to resemble an over-stuffed apartment his great-grandparents would have felt at home in. He certainly did. With so much cheap Victoriana available the transformation was not difficult to achieve. The family began referring to his room, with barbed affection, as The Parlour and his collection as 'cracked old pots', hoping he would swiftly pass through this errant phase and settle on more recognisable interests such as cars, space travel and swimming the Atlantic. But it rather pleased him to be different; when the phrase, 'Why can't you be more like other boys?' was dropped in his path, it made him firmer in his resolve to be more like himself. Why should he not derive extra pleasure from consuming tea and toast from his own old-fashioned tableware by candlelight? What was the problem with being as spiritual blotting paper primed to soak up the atmosphere and hold it in a malleable state to sweeten life as cream does strawberries? They were the components of a world he identified with and was acquiring knowledge of with an ease that didn't bless his schoolwork. His poor parents bewailed the fact that if he put as much time, thought and care into it as he did into The Parlour then he might not consistently remain bottom of the class.

His restless spirit brought to the arrangement and rearrangement of his collection a skill which, had it been in his maths book or in the gymnasium, would not have gone so unrecognised in the orthodox world. He would lie in bed supposed to be going to sleep and think, 'Those wax flowers in that glass dome and pair of vases might look better on that bookcase which would look better where that chest of drawers is.' He would be up in a trice, noiselessly resiting the Parlour's contents to maximise on harmony, a commodity achievable in a room setting but not always in life. It was not unknown for his mother, on entering later in the dark to tuck him up once he was asleep, to find herself embracing a plant stand or plaster statue. At her exasperated whisper, 'Well, where on earth *is* he?' he would often have to identify himself. On at least one occasion she abandoned trying to locate the bed altogether. Relatives and older family friends, heeding his weakness, occasionally favoured him with gifts born of their need to spring-clean attics. In turn they were accorded the highest accolade of a conducted tour of the collection with opinions invited as to the success of its latest arrangement.

The Parlour became more than simply a dust-trap; it provided that interactive continuity, in tune with the Avenues outside, which enabled the true self to prosper. The appeal of history's mellow repose (the only scholastic subject he received good marks for) and an interest in the times of idols such as Chopin, Dickens and Van Gogh led to a wider understanding: fashion, lighting, transport and social history of the period, not to mention furnishings and the decorative arts. If he wanted a portrait of one of them he would paint it, giving it the aged look with a coat or two from his father's shellac tin; if he wanted a gasolier to disguise his overhead electric light he would contrive one out of some lengths of copper piping, some feet of binding wire and half a dozen Woolworth's tumblers as glass shades.

He also felt that no self-respecting parlour was complete without a fireplace and hearth so, after copious references to the Adam style, he built one out of old bookshelves. He painted it white, then gave it a green marble effect with generous applications of water colour into which he rolled and dragged his handkerchief, much to his mother's annoyance. He painted a classical urn in the centre and made the basket grate out of a suitably adapted and blackened shoe box. Inside glowed a light bulb beneath red crepe paper and lumps of real coal borrowed from the coalhouse. Its elevation was further emphasised by the construction of an overmantel from pieces of plywood resting on the mantelshelf and stuck to the wall with Plasticine, his favourite adhesive. At the top he fixed a little shelf on which to place a seven-and-sixpenny bust of Mozart from Gough and Davy's music shop in Savile Street. Mock stone could be approximated by adding sand to emulsion paint and staining it the appropriate colour with the mortar lined in with a brush afterwards. A passing passion for Tudor brought these skills to the fore as did a line in papier-mâché bricks and plaster mouldings which, like the papier-mâché wood, received layers of paint before being treated to dirty washes for that authentic 'aged look'. Simulation of a panelled ceiling or walls required squares of brown wrapping paper and an infinity of gum strip.

What inviting comfort in which to be ill! Confined to his bed like a Pharaoh and his treasures in his tomb, he felt instantly better, particularly when he thought of school continuing without him. His winter ailments allowed him, for the only time, to have genuine heat in The Parlour provided by a cylindrical black paraffin stove on three bandy legs. To lie in bed, the blue-ribbed hot-water bottle at his feet, and see the steady warm glow illuminating the small red window on the side epitomized his sense of well-being. It was further enhanced by the kaleidoscopic patterns made by its adjustable top grille on the flat part of the ceiling. Having been forbidden to touch the stove, the first thing he did was to manipulate the projected images – quite different effects could be achieved on the ceiling's slope.

These assuring images are indissoluble with his mother's observation that what he needed was 'a good tonic to buck him up'. (Had she any idea of the ease with which he could leap in and out of bed, however poorly, when the passion took him?) The result of her observation was the unfailing appearance, from Podmore's, of a certain brown glass jar promising the delights of cod liver oil and malt, a toffee-like amalgam of glutinous mobility with which to stick precious days off school into memory's scrapbook, paperweights of barley sugar further to hold them in place. From these stolen moments flutter Robin's first attempts at serious poetry:

> One winter's night I took a torch
> To venture on the stair.
>   I quickly found, to my surprise,
> A boy who wasn't there.
>
> Short suddenly, then tall,
> Gross then almost thin,
>   We both met up and waved our arms
> Though I'd no fear of him

Blackly darting here and there
Then blankly not at all.
I'll take a torch tomorrow night
And send him up the wall.

Equally shadowy but none the less real was the pageant of characters, imaginary or authentic, who peopled The Parlour and its environment, acting out their agonies and ecstasies. Shirt collars could be turned up with a handkerchief issuing from the top button to simulate Beau Brummell's neckwear; trousers worn back-to-front approximated Regency smoothness; dressing gowns left open did well enough for frock coats; lengths of blackout material left over from the war swished and swirled as passable togas and highwaymen's cloaks; the bed made an ideal carriage for Napoleon to flee the field of Waterloo or the gig in which John Thurtell murdered William Weare by the October moonlight of 1824. Frequently piled with The Parlour's choicest objects, it rode the spumy breakers transporting the Swiss Family Robinson's possessions ashore after the shipwreck. The Parlour was amazingly versatile: it witnessed Pip's rescue of Miss Havisham from the flames in Satis House's dusty twilight (closed curtains, candles and liberal sprinklings of talcum powder essential here); it converted easily into Buckingham Palace or Jack the Ripper's Whitechapel slum.

The family were prudent in not interfering with these activities. Aware of occasional thumps and bangs from overhead, they wisely continued with their kitchen duties, reconciled with the knowledge that the boy upstairs was completely loopy. On occasions he found he had the whole house to himself, the family, despite its doubts about his mental state, happy to entrust him with some responsibility. The ample staircase and wide landings gave a new dimension to life's dramas; it is not commonly known that the Prince Regent attended a levée up the Grand Staircase of 25, Park Avenue or that Queen Marie Antoinette of France descended it on the way to her guillotining in the back garden.

★ ★ ★ ★ ★

As Robin thinks himself into the 1950s, one other radiance persists, illumined with an enchantment difficult to appreciate when faced with the contemporary brash universality of media culture. The style of early television's monochrome, coarse-grained, leisurely flickering seems hidebound and innocent in the light of current thrusting multi-coloured, multi-competitive bombardments of frenetic hype more explicit than reality itself.

Back in 1953, though, only a few years after the service had resumed transmission after the war, it was doubtful whether black and white television – or THE television as it was referred to – was a serious enough undertaking to be allowed into Westminster Abbey to relay Queen Elizabeth's solemn

Drawn from memory: The parlour complete with insulating tape lattice and later plastic crystal chandelier.

Coronation to her realm. Only 2 million households owned a television receiver and, though the largest screen was only 14 inches square, (36cm), it was thought less decadent, when not being viewed, to shut it in a cabinet behind closed doors as if it were a guilty secret. Maurice's family had no secret to hide, not because they scorned decadence but rather that there simply was not the money in the household exchequer for such a luxury. But the Coronation represented the values and aspirations of a nation newly out of crisis; and, once the Queen agreed that her dedication to that nation should be shared through the medium of television, sales of receivers increased.

As luck would have it, Maurice was given one by a grateful business customer, Mr. Harman of Autowreckers on Clough Road, whose fortune was accelerated by dealing in smashed-up vehicles. It was round his gift of a walnut-veneered 12-inch EKCO without doors, retailing at £69 in the shops, that the immediate neighbourhood clustered that rainy June day to drink and munch their way through the sacred ceremony, presented as if from a silver salver by Sylvia Peters and Richard Dimbleby.

Robin found himself easily influenced by the new dimension this visual stimulation brought to his life each week. The sense of occasion, which the family viewed together as a unit, was enhanced by the limited transmission hours of the single BBC television channel. It began at 3 p.m. on weekdays and 5 p.m. on Sundays. Children's Television occupied the hours from 5 p.m. to 6 p.m., when the transmitters were switched off until 7 p.m. to give the announcers time to change into faultless evening dress for a 3½-hour marathon until bedtime. Televiewing was schemed into the evenings' activities – its selective availability heightening the sense of occasion.

Any programmes connected with history, art or music gave him ideas for life in The Parlour, particularly the adaptations of Dickens and other period classics, all broadcast live with every blemish and flaw. Wobbly sets, unintended glimpses of studio equipment and a fragile shell of illusion were no deterrent to his sense of belief. From the first transmission of any of Dickens's works, *The Pickwick Papers* of 1952, the illusions created for a wide audience were only a larger scale version of illusions he created for himself and were just as valid. Many of his ideas were engendered and supported by the way his imagination imbued the small-scale black and white images with a colourful dimension way beyond the cathode ray tube.

★ ★ ★ ★ ★

'I shouldn't like you to think,' he said with a sudden attack of conscience, 'that though the most real people for me existed only in my imagination, I had no contact with living human beings. I did have friends of my own age – children who lived locally – with whom I played quite amicably. I enjoyed, in fact, the contrast between them and me. They were necessary in order to throw my world into relief though it was often a relief to throw them back into theirs. But I was prepared to allow none outside the family into my personal world which The Parlour represented. I knew it was illusory but I also knew it was necessary to the building of my life and well-being – to cushion but offset, to console but inspire, to contain but express. It never occurred to me as bizarre that I should find it necessary to create an environment which was theatrical and false. Nor does it now all these years later. In fact, I was doing then what people are now paid good money for doing in the media and elsewhere: recreating the period look indoors and out, cherishing bygones, appraising each others' antiques whether on roadshows or not, faking marble and distressing paint. The Californian-born Dennis Severs has even created his own living history environment in his Spitalfields home at 18, Folgate Street, north-east of St. Paul's Cathedral. *His* passion for candles and complete indifference to power cuts has become a business based on dispensing with modern conveniences and letting the past speak for itself. He also has learned not to let too much light in on the

A tree for all seasons: the silver birch's assuring presence.

magic. Like Siegfried Sassoon and me, he's happy in his craving to revisit the past and give the modern world the slip. To those mortals who gape in perplexity his motto is, 'You either see it or you don't.' I, for one, do see it and probably perplex others because of it. Call it pastiche, interior and garden make-over, installation art or just plain second-hand existence, I could now be a millionaire if I'd had a strong marketing strategy, an acute business head and a good agent.'

After I had given a tactful time for this passionate little homily to sink in, I said to Robin that, so far, he had been dealing with the potential claustrophobia of indoors and a stuffy overcrowded indoors at that, however much he loved it. His use of the word garden reminded me of one of the glories of 25 and I said so.

Twenty feet wide, just over seven metres, it stretched back for 150 feet, (45 metres). It contained a variety of mature trees and greenery which, in conjunction with the surrounding wealth of nature and birdsong, gave it the appeal of open countryside. It backed onto the gardens of Westbourne Avenue, given scale by two exalted poplars at the left-hand corner. There was lilac too, laburnum, pairs of apple and plum, any amount of privet, broom, elderflower, with beeches, sycamores and ash burgeoning in green plumes, thrown up as if by some vital discharge of nature. Most becoming of all, a gracious silver birch as high as the house feathered a corner of the lawn in shimmering sweeps. Here was the soul of the garden, as the fireplace was the soul of The Parlour. Singing birds clamoured the generous spaces, a welter of daytime choruses gradually giving way to the lingering resonance of late blackbird or thrush duetting with the limpid Angelus bell echoing from the French Convent School chapel in Park Grove.

> In this seasonable land,
> I tell of a garden, greenly strewn,
> Where sentinel poplars stand
> To mark and keep
> The place I grew to know and love
> So soon:
>   A leisured band
>   Of grass and growing generousness,
>   Of hushed ways deep
>   Within the glare and gloom
>   Of night and noon,
> Where my youthful heart's impetuousness
> Charged me with a love
> Of every corner, part and plan,
> Every scent and sound. Each reminds me,
>   Now I am a man,
> Of myself amongst such succulence.

I see azure larkspur, cream convolvulus
Opening to the amber flood of dawn;
Star-clustered loosestrife's yellow regiments
Parading the guardian wall;
Lady's mantle, monkshood; the ox-eye daisy
Spangling the polished grasses pointing the morn;
The keen merge of coriander, fennel, thyme;
The drowsy peonies' splendour
Heavy over noon-dried edges of the lawn;
Tender drifts of lilac, rose and pink –
Of night-scented stock along the dusky gravel walk.

I know it well – so well.
I know it all – each pebble, tuft and space,
Each tiny mood, each new dimension
On its seasoned face.
It holds me – will not relinquish
Until I become subservient to its power
And have committed all that I am
As if I were its willing slave.
Yet, well I know,
    By each increasing hour,
How few human intensities endure
    With so comfortable and safe repose
Without turning sour.

At the end of the lawn and more cultivated part of the garden clustered
irises and golden rod bordering a rougher more neglected area once covered
with chicken houses. A profusion of mouldy bricks and wood provided the
raw materials for den-building and hideouts doubling as camps or castles.
This patch of secret delights, being out of sight and sound of the house, became
the outdoor equivalent of The Parlour. Some of the wood went towards a
tree-house in the long-suffering silver birch, but the majority serviced the
roof of a three-sided brick shack economically utilising partial walls edging a
sand pit his father had built for him after the war. The fourth side, open to the
westerly elements, was hung with two large rubber ex-army groundsheets
fixed by nails to the ceiling crossbar. To open up, one merely furled them
over onto the roof outside and secured them with bricks.

But The Shack was best all closed in – mysterious – slightly damp and
earthy, with an exclusivity about its frayed light, not to say its lowness, making
intrusion by grown-ups unlikely and hard on their joints. Here you could
make yourself sick on a penny cigarette from the shop on the corner of
Newland Avenue, or make your own from grass cuttings rolled in brown
paper. Both were revolting but adult, even if they did smoke The Shack out,
sting eyes and throats and put one off from being adult.

A good blaze warms The Shack.

The greatest asset to this des. res. was a working fireplace and chimney, an inspired adaptation of some of the hollow blocks from the dismantled air-raid shelter saved for the garden at Maurice's request. Now that the blocks were empty of sand and piled one on top of another, the smoke had clear access away from the hearth with The Shack warming up like a proper room. A mantelshelf secured above the opening provided an altar for candles and those special little treasures equalling household gods without which life is pretty arid. In Robin's case they had to include a plaster bust of whichever composer he happened to have a crush on at the time. Turns were taken for the democratic enjoyment of being nearest this wondrous source of heat just as it was for the position by the only window – a gap in the wall harbouring a piece of glass stolen from a rubbish pile in a safely distant ten-foot.

But no household gods went beyond The Shack, for the remaining land was the main venue for action of a more physical kind. It had the added advantage of a large black garden shed, home to Marion's guinea pigs, Ruby, Stripey and Beauty. It was also where she kept her petrol-driven bicycle called the Phut-phut; many a reluctant camp fire had been coaxed into life by a siphon system from its fuel tank.

Like The Parlour with its cracked old pots and hideous vases, this back lot was versatile enough to double as a stage set, television studio or film location. Scenes would be rehearsed, then shot, their actors followed by a camera made from a grocery box with a loo-roll projecting as a lens and a boom mike formed by hanging a tin on the end of a clothes prop. This gave much of the action a reason for being: Napoleon's flaming torchlight retreat from Moscow through nightly snow, the escape of Mary Queen of Scots from Loch Leven castle in thick fog, the Battle of Waterloo in thick rain and in thick sun, anything to do with cowboys, Davy Crockett, pirates or the Swiss Family Robinson setting up their new island home.

A theatre could be contrived by stretching clothes lines across the lawn and setting the stage behind lengths of ubiquitous blackout material clothes-pegged along for curtains. With assorted chairs forming the auditorium in front, the local populace was invited to witness the latest dramatic presentation in the hope of moving the neighbourhood and critics to a hurricane of acclaim.

His parents welcomed their son's contact with normal children of his own age in the hope that they would knock the corners off some of his more extreme flights of fancy. The most enduring presence was Jamie from opposite, a little older but a willing comrade in boyish secrets and participant in make-believe of a more manly kind. He brought a healthy modern approach to the collaboration. There was much sinking of submarines, blowing up of tanks and bridges as well as combat situations involving fire, water and assorted missiles best left unseen by gardeners, householders and the Armed Forces, of which his father was a member.

The solid but rickety end fence and sprouts of hedging bore the stresses and scorches of many an enthusiastic blaze which had added a touch of realism to baronial hall or outlaws' camp. Many were the tins of mud boiled, shaken and stirred as venison or poacher's broth; many the beetles cooked on tin lids to be passed off as undreamed-of delicacies. The guinea pigs, however held no appeal.

One December dusk after coming indoors from a notably gruelling afternoon robbing the rich and giving to the poor, his mother, chancing to glance the length of the garden as she drew the sitting room curtains, casually remarked that the bonfire seemed to be going rather well but wasn't it a bit near the shed, dear? Half a glance was enough to confirm that it *was* the shed. All hands to the hose saved the Phut-phut and guinea pigs from an explosive situation but not Robin's backside from even warmer treatment. Out came the long thin cane reserved for his worst offences, his father's ample lap providing his bed of pain. With the words 'damn good thrashing' stinging his ears and *gluteus maximus,* the Outlaw of Sherwood was forbidden to rape, loot and pillage for the foreseeable future.

It was at such times that all the imagined injustices in the universe seemed heaped on the jumble sale of his life with no one, least of all his parents, understanding the complexities of his suffering mind and body. How could they be expected to know what true suffering was and how painful it could be to be so misunderstood? It was then that he wished he could escape into the blue Italian landscapes on his Parlour's cracked old tea set. Barely able to sit down, the distraught poet, in afflicted passion, resorted to penning verses of recrimination and retribution. He hoped this would cause his parents to feel guilty about their cruelty to him and driving him to consider running away or suicide.

ADOLESCENT DESPAIR
(over-reaction to a minor admonishment)

What hellish creatures are these
That torture souls
And turn hopes of light
Into fears and screaming agonies?

Dupes! Deceivers of life!
Why haunt the heart
That bleeds and tears
To cry with blistered voice
To save the rays of hope?

Black, black indeed
The outlook reigns;
No hope of clarity abides –
Only fear of obscured shapes
Slinking in a foggy vision's shadow.

Oh Devil! You who sting us with these ghouls!
Take them from their sucking grip
And let them perish
With the growls
Of all their bloody bitterness.

His mother, on being treated to this saturated melodrama, declared that
her son was either a bloody fool or a bloody genius.

INTERLUDE

In our younger days when blood flowed thicker and faster, centrally heated houses, particularly older ones, were considered something of an unconventional luxury; central heating was for public buildings and one of the more friendly aspects of school. Householders took for granted that open coal fires were the central source of heat – that electric and gas fires supplemented the comfort zone – that doors to rooms needed to be kept closed in order to conserve heat and that rooms needed to be heated only when in use, an economical dictum also applying to lighting. Number 25, being a long, thin house with draughty passages downstairs and up, was no different and for at least eight months of the year was selectively temperate.

But that was the way things were; feeling cold meant you simply put on more clothes. The only time Robin remembers his parents lighting the gas fire in their bedroom was while they dressed in evening attire before attending some function. This extravagant indulgence would be accompanied by a glass of sherry each, leaving the room with that warm after-presence of the fruit of the vine, cleanliness and scent – exotic tasters of a grown-up world. He remembers no fire ever in the nursery but the ritual of blazing coals in the downstairs rooms bringing the house instantly alive, particularly the study. The polished glow on mahogany and blushed half-lights crimsoning white walls and ceiling behind snugly drawn curtains epitomised the well-being of Christmas – of sitting cross-legged on the Turkey red carpet leaning his back against the wall in his favourite corner. Before him rested the cigar box, pale green lustre part of his private worship of seasonal anticipation and fruition.

Regardless of whether The Parlour was an ice-box or oven, hours were spent over the years absorbed in its attractions, the heat (or lack of it) part of the very spirit of the moment. The drawings of period rooms in Osbert Lancaster's book *Homes Sweet Homes,* and the photos of room settings in his own growing library collection merged with the reality of his own space and attempts to imitate what he saw.

And whilst reading in bed at night before the older generation had retired, how familiar became the clatter of supper's preparation in the kitchen beneath him, the inviting rattle of the laden trolley along to the sitting room. Though Madeleine cooked three meals a day for the family they still demanded her *pièce de résistance:* coffee, cheeses, fruit, home-made patisserie, of which an extremely clarty ginger cake was obligatory – no one would consider it unless it was over-treacled and under-cooked. Little wonder she said that she always felt chained to the gas stove and kitchen sink.

But then, in the replete moments before the outposts of bed, she and Maurice would relax at the upright piano, a bright but mellow Evestaff piled with sheet music, some of it Maurice's manuscript compositions. Amongst his many accomplishments he had taught himself the mechanics of harmony and counter-point and to sight-read to a fair degree. He enjoyed the intellectual challenge of their disciplines. Madeleine, having studied as a youngster with Mrs. Russell Starr, one of Hull's leading teachers, was a more intuitive musician. She adored Chopin in particular who was much to Robin's taste. He would fall asleep serenaded by nocturnes and some of the quieter *Preludes* sharing the upward journey to The Parlour. As they floated him into the cradle of Morpheus, the yearning harmonies under-playing ripples of finger work in Christian Sinding's *Rustle of Spring* encapsulated life at 25, its flavour, its immutability.

V

PERSONALITIES

His own parents, he that had father'd him and she that had . . . birth'd him,
They gave this child more of themselves than that,
They gave him afterward every day, they became part of him.

Walt Whitman.
Leaves of Grass.

In 1955 Maurice was 50 and newly promoted to the managership of the Midland Bank in Paragon Square, Hull. With high moral conscience he took naturally to his many business and social commitments becoming a respected and wise figure from whom one was happy to seek sound advice and help. His dramatic, broadcasting and production gifts with amateur theatre continued to absorb his leisure hours as well as interests in music, electronics and the wonders of wireless and the new age of television.

Under his versatile but deceptively unassuming manner there fermented a creative heart every bit as passionate as his young son's but kept under better control; his life was governed by his motto, 'Never let your heart rule your head', a dictum Robin found impossible to follow. One gained the impression, in line with Maurice's Ariean birth sign, that 'father knows best' – frustrating at times as with the best of intentions, he would tend to take over if asked for a little assistance with something. Robin was inclined to hold back for fear of being swamped by his all-knowing ability, aware that his father and brother had a grown-up relationship with much in common. But with Robin's well-

The grandparents' dog, Simon, joins the family pose, 1953.

being at heart there was nothing he was not prepared to do for him, as with the rest of the family. He took particular interest in his music and writing, encouraging a love of the written and spoken word. As they grew older, he benefited from his father's wisdom and learned much from his sense of literary style, discussion of ideas and visits to each other's desks in an easy working accord.

His father spiced his conversation with a fund of little phrases. If he had impressed him with some achievement it would be, 'My Godfrey Daniel – I take my hat off to you,' but nobody knew Godfrey's identity and never thought to ask – like the concept of God he just Was. If he considered that Robin was behaving particularly badly he would ask whether he was 'setting his stall out to annoy your mother and me'. There was no answer to this as Robin was not conscious of having a stall *to* set out; and if cheek or rudeness had besmirched the atmosphere he would threaten to 'knock your block off', meaning his head. More than once Robin was told that his father and mother were seriously worried about him, as though it were possible to be worried unseriously. In connection with academic studies, always a sore point, he was bidden to 'work like stink' and not 'fritter his time away', otherwise he would 'come to a sticky end'. But the one which said it all was the head-shake accompanied by the bemused observation, 'I sometimes wonder who you think you are.' There was no answer to this as Robin had yet to find that out for himself.

As his mother established her identity after Nanny's departure a wise, fair and efficient relationship strengthened the growing process. She had a natural social honesty, put others above herself and was completely above affectation. She also had the rare gift of determination to make the best of everything no matter how unpleasant, even at the expense of becoming harassed and exhausted. Having Mediterranean blood inherited from her Greek Dermond father, she was prone to being volatile, followed by spells of nervous illness making her irritable. She took her duties as the wife of one of Hull's businessmen extremely seriously, tending to subjugate herself, both emotionally and creatively, to his lead like a true Piscean. This was not because she lacked a strong character but rather the reverse. It gave her the strength, coupled with a loving sense of duty, to cope with timed demands of a working marriage and family. She deferred to him on all major issues and depended on him for financial security, housekeeping and dress allowance – somewhat outdated concepts by modern standards of equality, but Maurice was Master of the House. Perhaps part of her nervous condition stemmed from suppression of her artistic and creative gifts by his well-intended benevolence.

She, too, had her web of phrases. Her favourite was, 'I always seem to be working with a pistol to my head', meaning that she had too much to do in too short a time. When fatigued by her own high standards she would groan, 'I don't know why I flagellate myself.' Again, if some unexpected occurrence cropped up to deflect or hinder her in her routine she would exclaim, 'I have had my morning (or afternoon) taken from me!' as if her handbag had been snatched in the street. She found it almost impossible to delegate.

A hardened greyish spinster doctor who had been keen on Maurice during his courting days and lost out to Madeleine once told her, to her face, that she had tried her hardest to dislike her but had found she simply couldn't. The family took their cue from their father whose whole being so obviously existed for her benefit and welfare, with a loving warmth as taken for granted as day following night. Until the morning he died he kept in his wallet next to his heart the two-page letter she wrote him in 1928 expressing her feelings at accepting his proposal of marriage.

Robin was fortunate in being raised within the security of such a family team. Though his older sister and brother were pursuing their own careers, they tolerated most of his juvenile difficulties with affectionate patience. Attractive characters in their own right, with unerring senses of responsibility, they represented the maturity it was hoped their errant brother would achieve given enough example and not a little encouragement.

So worried had Marion been about him that at roughly the same time she secretly sought advice from a child psychologist family friend:

> ... There is no doubt that he is a problem child in a way, but at the same time there is no doubt that he is himself faced with a problem situation, and that the problems he presents are, in fact, the ways by which he is trying to solve them.
>
> The child born when the rest of the family is growing up and when the parents are middle-aged has to face a very mixed situation. He is in a sense an only child. At the same time he is the baby. Either of these carries its own difficulties, but he has to face them – to do something about them – to escape. This may happen in reality or simply into a world of his own – a retreat into a fantasy where he day-dreams or lives out a positive drama of his own.
>
> Here you can help Robin gain *legitimate* and *satisfactory* compensation in a way that is acceptable to the family, for he is particularly lucky in being not only part of a creative and cultural environment but also himself having rich possibilities – through his drawing and painting, his music and dramatic ability; and since he cannot really share the grown-ups' interests, it is important that they should share his *at his level*: appreciation of his achievements when he has made the effort – appreciation of his independent and refreshing (and indeed unique) approach (eg. music) and 'soft pedalling' on adult demands. Adverse criticism emphasising his helplessness is likely to turn him away from the very ways by which he may work out his own salvation ...
>
> Therefore, as his sister, help him to feel that what he does *in his own way* matters. What he has in his own room may give you ideas as to how he can be helped. Find practical ways in which he can legitimately feel he is becoming more independent, self reliant and skilful. If you can project yourself imaginatively and sympathetically into his situation, you'll find some measure of success. He is equal to any of your patients in need of 'nursing care'.

Marion did much to engineer a more enlightened attitude and throughout the normal growing pains of youth a desired improvement became noticeable.

★ ★ ★ ★ ★

Robin, Marion, Peter and Simon.

This coincided with Maurice seeking an improvement in his wife's well-being. He encouraged her to employ a succession of approved domestics after Nanny had gone to help ease the burden of running the house; some of them lived-in during the week. There was Nella whose parade of grown-up daughters seemed constantly visiting; then came Margaret whose capable jollity made her invaluable for bedtime story-reading; Edna who was stone deaf, engaged through the Institute for the Deaf on Spring Bank of which Maurice was, for many years, Chairman of the Board of Management and Madeleine a member of the Ladies' Advisory Committee. She became known as 'Loving Edna' after the way she signed herself in her Christmas cards.

Robin never remembered 'Haggy Aggy's' correct name after he christened her the worst insult he could come up with. So hopelessly unsuited to her employment she lasted barely a handful of weeks, but in spite of his animosity towards her, begged to be allowed another chance as she had nowhere else to go. Sobbing onto a large red glass brooch pinned to her overcoat, she and her battered suitcase were shown kindly but firmly out of the front door much to his relief.

From then on his mother employed only 'dailies' who came to 'do' for her. The nicest and most able was Joan, who stayed several years until, aged nearly 40, she found she was expecting a third child. She had an endearing way of stating the obvious; on Robin's return from school each day she would say, 'Oh, have you come?' as if it were a huge surprise; on his leaving it would be,

'Oh, are you going?' One had only to climb the stairs or play the piano to be asked if that's what your were doing. She too sobbed on departure but for different reasons: she said that his mother was the only employer she had ever worked for who treated her like a lady.

Throughout this mixed baggage of domestic activity, one pearl of great price slopped her way through 25 with mop and bucket to 'do' once a week. Jane Anne Locke was at least 106, clad in wrap-around print overall, thick brown wrinkled stockings with a mind of their own when it came to obeying the law of gravity and spare grey hair scraped into a wispy bun. Her single tooth in her upper gum fitted nicely beside the single tooth in her lower gum when her mouth was closed. This was not very often as she would hum her way through her cleaning and keep up a running commentary throughout the house telling the contents what she was doing to them, with what and why. She had an aversion to replacing anything in its rightful position as well as being incapable of putting plugs back in sockets after vacuuming. It took a week to put the house to rights before she arrived for the next disturbance. But she was happy with the extra money two hours at 25 provided having been taken on there as an act of kindness via a neighbour for whom she also, one assumes, provided equally eccentric services.

The Parlour Madeleine let none of her daily helps into for fear of them giving notice. Robin was quite content with this arrangement as he preferred being custodian of his own dust and cobwebs. It always intrigued him that for all the amusement his purchase of second-hand goods caused, his parents seemed to have forgotten that they had done exactly the same thing when they were economy-conscious newlyweds. Nor was his mother occasionally averse to borrowing some of his purchases with which to augment her dinner parties – a silver-plated cruet was in particular demand along with a gadrooned entrée dish and five-branch candelabrum.

On either side of 25 lived members of the scholastic profession who did their best to give him extra coaching in arithmetic and English in order to equip him for twice failing the entrance exam to Hymers College. On the right was a large elderly retired headmistress with asthma. Her valiant efforts were smothered by B.O. in her morbid dining room where her pupil gasped to be let out into the fresh air. Occasionally she came round to operate in his father's study, an unwise locality given its manifold distractions.

On the left, to balance the educative scales, there lurked the unretired headmaster of a local Secondary school. He was small and spare, like a weathered gargoyle, with a smudge of moustache like Hitler's and nervous, spasmodic double-barrelled cough. His proximity was thus easy to detect, which made free time in the garden something to be engineered. As likely as not he would otherwise have Robin round at his place working out the area of his lawn or circumference of his flower beds, to say nothing of the square root of his pear tree. He did his best, in a needling sort of way, making occasional forays into the complexities of the English language for which

Robin showed some aptitude. In the end he had to call a truce as his persistent cough showed signs of aggravation. He did, however, succeed in fostering Robin's ability to harden his heart and close his mind to anything which threatened his sense of freedom and well-being exemplified by where he lived – a haven for all eventualities. These two watchtowers of self-defence were as invaluable to him as the dazzling nuggets of chandelier glass in their shabby cigar box.

A couple of doors away at 21 lived Mrs. Charter, an elderly widow perpetually dressed in brown satin and low hems. Her husband may have been Charles Charter the Estate Agent. She was of the same era but would have exchanged life in Victoria Avenue for that in Park Avenue. Whether this had been the case or not, she was delighted with the polite young man from 25, periodically inviting him into her brown front room to choose a brown toffee from a brown tin. She enjoyed his playing of her stout piano, sitting in a brown study as he filled her fern-fringed collection of sleekly polished furniture and gold-framed watercolours of Victorian Devon with swells of dated sound. She was as soft and sweet as a toffee herself, often to be heard singing and talking to the birds and occasionally bumping into things with little murmurs of surprise. All this was explained when she had a fall and Maurice answered her 'phone call for help. He and Marion went round to deal with her. They were unable to get her immediately into bed after flinging back the bedding due to the avalanche of gin bottles.

Some friends of Robin's parents lodged with a similar veteran at 70, Westbourne Avenue, a gaunt pile even browner than Mrs. Charter's but with a greater absence of light caused by a surfeit of dark furnishings. Throughout the passage of time and two world wars it had managed to retain its original gas lighting. The Misses Lillian and Adena Carter had probably resided in this living history site since it was built but now only Miss Adena was left alone in its cold echoing chambers, happy to rent some of them out. Swathed in black and jet, with a blotchy face wizened like a date in a drought, she had no concept of how she scared Robin – not enough, though, to stop his requesting her to demonstrate the lighting of her globed gasolier and wall brackets in the only room she seemed to inhabit at the back of the house overlooking the over-shady garden. His awesome fascination graduated to the upstairs, riddled with bedrooms lumbered with gleaming mahogany, faded pictures and marble washstands bearing china jugs and bowls which had been in constant use since she was a girl. Most challenging to the nerve was a visit to the upstairs toilet which necessitated carrying a lighted candle, usually one of life's chief pleasures. Here, though, it invariably blew out in the draught halfway along the passage leaving nothing for company but the whispering rattle of a nearby bead curtain. Or was it the ghost of her long-dead sister swishing along the polished linoleum?

Number 25 was surrounded by well established characters: Cecil Mason at 15, a quiet, dapper old gent in gold-rimmed spectacles and tweed plus-fours whose wife was the hearty reverse, talking and laughing loudly as her rolling gait propelled her along the pavement like a cauldron in a high wind. Her voice came out in enthusiastic gusts as did that of Mrs. Parsons, hammering the unwary into the ground and finishing off the job with a pneumatic drill of a laugh. Miss Davy lent a certain proper dignity to the area as she pedalled her sit-up-and-beg bicycle whilst in firm control of her umbrella held high overhead. Simon Goldberg the artist lived a few doors further on from 25.

Across the Avenue lived the Hoggarts and the Goodmans at 26 and 28. As well as being family friends both had children who augmented the local gang centred round Robin and Jamie, trooping in and out of each other's gardens to do whatever it is gangs do in each other's gardens. Simon Hoggart was later to become a writer and radio personality and Roy Goodman a professional musician of outstanding integrity with an international reputation. Mary, his mother, Hull's leading peripatetic string teacher, was a familiar sight weaving her bicycle amongst the city traffic instrument case strapped to her back.

When Robin had been about seven, his parents asked him if he would like to learn to play the piano properly, obviously intrigued by his extempore attempts to emulate Liszt and Rachmaninov at their most flamboyant.

'No thank you,' he had replied. 'I can play already.' He was nevertheless packed off each week to 28, where Roy's father, Peter Goodman, Head of Music at Kingston High School and the City Organist, soon proved he could not. For musical theory he was taken on by the sister of John Joubert, the contemporary composer and Professor of Music at Hull University. At his upright piano in Park Grove she did her best, but, as she seemed adversely critical of any music not by Bach or Bartok (and presumably Joubert), the sessions became rather flat, pupil and teacher rarely in tune.

The Hoggarts had their front room knocked through to the back one which was Mr. Hoggart's study, for Robin would see him through the front window sometimes working at his lamp lit desk. He realised afterwards that he must have been engaged on his groundbreaking and scholarly study of the modern cultural climate, *The Uses of Literacy,* first published in 1957. It thrilled him to think he had seen a real living author at work on books to be bought in shops. The fact that Richard Hoggart was also Senior Staff Tutor in Literature in the Department of Adult Education at the University was of secondary importance, just as his own father's literary and dramatic pursuits were more significant than his banking managerships.

The Hull poet Philip Larkin, another toiler at the University, lived in an upstairs flat at the Princes Avenue end of Pearson Park. Though Robin was unaware at the time, he has since wondered if Larkin loved the trees as much as he did. His high windows placed him virtually in a tree-house up near the crown of those mighty chestnuts under which children played by the lake. The Park with its timeless atmosphere of enclosed repose swayed the younger poet's sensibilities with *Family Tea:*

In 1891 we were a family of eight:
    Mama, Papa, Tom and Henry,
    Charlotte, Michael, Robert
And Kate.
Our house, solid and new, was white
    With a green front door and porch
        Full of leaves –
The second along on the right
    From the park-keeper's lodge
        With a clock on the wall
            Near the eaves
And tall iron gate.

In 1958 I was seventy-three.
    The youngest.
Our home is still white
    With a green front door.
But one place only is set
At the family dining table for tea:
    Tom and Henry fell long ago in the field,
    Michael and Robert at sea;
    Charlotte wasted in childbirth,
        Leaving a still house, memories,
And me.

Other figures with a wider reputation used Park Avenue as their base. The actor John Woodnutt, then with the Hull Repertory Company at the New Theatre, lodged directly opposite 25. He was unmistakable as he owned the only vehicle in the vicinity – a vintage London taxi in dark blue with a soft top, running boards and bulbous honking horn. He added a touch of swaggering glamour to the retiring area much as Mr. Toad would had his motoring craze lasted. Glamour of a more volatile kind accompanied a Brylcreemed Cliff Richard early in his career as he came out on his first major tour of England. Whilst at the Regal Cinema next to Paragon Station, word got out that he was staying somewhere in Park Avenue with the result that the small hours of the morning were punctuated by flurries of high-pitched feminine enthusiasm and the constant ringing of 25's door bell, the prelude to eager but confused groups asking if Cliff was in. His true locale at 22 with Mrs. Baillie was never officially divulged by the neighbourhood but Cliff was tracked down, resulting in her front garden being trampled to death. The rumour even circulated that she had made a fortune by ripping up his bed sheets and selling the fragments to fans.

In addition is the roll-call of actors, writers, film directors and public figures whose lives, at some stage, have been touched by the Avenues, from Joseph Groves Boxhall, Fourth Officer on the *Titanic* at 27, Westbourne, and Amy

Johnson the aviatrix at 85, Park Avenue, to Ian Carmichael, film and television actor, at 32, Westbourne, where he remembers the polished shire horses pulling the Corporation dustcarts beneath dappled chestnuts.

A pair of Westbourne Avenue gardens abutted the end of 25's, divided by the stalwart but scarred five-foot fence which continually bore the brunt of juvenile games and more than once suffered the same fiery fate as the black shed. One of the gardens was owned by a woman whose name Robin and the Outlaws never knew but whose bad temper from over the fence created hatred in the hearts of those who caused it. She reminded the raucous, irritating gang of a disagreeable tortoise whose frowning expression remained her most noticeable feature, along with her backside. It projected permanently into the air as she bent over, incessantly gardening, earning her the most. extreme order of contempt with which they could invest her – Mrs. Bottom. Her apple tree, gnarled and twisted like its owner, overhung the fence near the black shed, once a year depositing its hefty green cookers into the Outlaws' territory. Windfalls would soon turn a squashy cidery brown which, when stuck with a few small twigs, converted into unique bombs or land mines. Jamie was very enthusiastic about these. What a gorgon Mrs. Bottom could be, particularly if she caught an Outlaw actually lobbing his missile onto her lawn where it would gratifyingly explode like an alcoholic cow-pat.

The second abutting garden belonged to Miss Hannchen Drasdo, a woman of towering presence, voice and personality, her ear-lobes weighted down like divers' boots with pendulous swinging earrings, her flat feet largely and sensibly encased. She was another friend of Robin's parents through their joint association with the City's amateur theatricals. The Outlaws did not set out *deliberately* to annoy her but she somehow remained suspicious. It worked both ways, for, as soon as they heard her carrying cadences the other side of the fence, they were keen to be seen behaving themselves. Many an industrious-looking occupation was pulled out of the hat at short notice when her presence was in the offing. They no more thought of annoying Miss Drasdo than they did of not annoying Mrs. Bottom. The odd thing was that they respected any rumbling chastisement they received from her. She was saved from contempt by their appreciation of her fundamental humanity and underlying, often barely concealed, sense of humour. She even once obligingly extinguished the flaming fence with her watering can whilst watched by an apprehensive cluster of small boys. She did it with as much calm grace as if it had been a perfectly natural part of everyday gardening duties. What impressed Robin most was that there was no dramatic, 'Wait until your father hears about this!' As far as he knew Miss Drasdo kept the secret.

Yet in spite of many a game she ruined, he remembers her with affectionate gratitude. Once, whilst admiring a particularly fine white Parian bust of Beethoven she owned, she hooted in clipped stentorian tones, 'He shall be yours one day when you are older.' Young as he was, he knew people sometimes said things on the spur of the moment they did not mean and would soon forget. The following week, however, she sent him an envelope inscribed, MAY HE BRING YOU PLEASURE. Inside, to his great surprise, was a bronze bust of Beethoven three inches (8cm) high. He wrote her a thank-you letter hoping she had not felt she *ought* to give him something. His father assured him that she was made of sterner stuff than that.

When he was nearing 20 she came to see the family not long before she died. She handed him a brown paper parcel.

'I promised you this,' she thundered. 'I know you'll look after him.' As the white Beethoven emerged like one of his own melodies Robin's sense of gratitude was impossible to express. What moved him most was that she had taken him seriously without question and kept her promise. It stood him in good stead years later as a schoolmaster when he evaluated the importance of never making promises to pupils he would not or could not keep. Beethoven remains on his writing desk to this day, testimony to his previous owner's disqualification from the apple bomb hit-list.

★ ★ ★ ★ ★

A constant source of entertainment at 25 was the variety of male species his sister attracted over the worn sandstone step. She had developed into an elegant reliant figure with a winning smile which enhanced her natural gifts of helping others and making them feel better for having seen her. Her dedication to working in a caring capacity covering a wide range of medical, social and civic activities would one day be celebrated in the award of an M.B.E. She also had a reserved side – even shy, but led a moderately gregarious life, acquiring the reputation between her teasingly irreverent brothers of existing on equal doses of shopping, parties and rests in bed.

There was Desperate Dave, short and bluff, with flat hat and battered white van; Rolly Ron with nothing vehicular to boast of save the spare tyres round his chin and midriff; Statuesque Stuart with mock leopard skin cladding round his Wolseley's steering wheel and a laugh like a tractor starting up. Pukkah Piers, smoothly coated with Public School charm, blasé with champers and binocs, beetling down to Beverley Races. He was the only one who matched the suavity of Anthony Steel, the cinema idol whom she rather admired.

Then there was Pip, a brawny horticulturalist who showered her and her mother with hothouse blooms until they ran out of vases. A most persistent candidate this, pursuing a hopelessly one-sided enthusiasm, completely impervious to the heaviest hints. In the roll-call of Marion's achievements it was unique to see her leap like an acrobat through the French windows to the garden in an attempt to avoid one of her admirers. She had also been known, in tighter moments, to effect her escape through Peter's bedroom window and gain access to the garden by the way of the outside toilet's roof and a jump of some feet into a clump of irises. The cabaret was sadly aborted when her father stepped in to have a manly word with Pip before Marion ruined any more plants.

Peter in characteristic attitude with a screwdriver.

Peter, cheery, good-natured and something of a hero in his younger brother's eyes, had laid claim to the room next to his both physically and volubly, for it contained the wire-strewn evidence of his passion for amateur radio and electronic equipment, none of which worked without some degree of noise. The room, 12-foot square with garden view and window seat, was a jungle of cables, condensers, resisters, coils, humming loud speakers, blinking lights, flashings, bleepings, squeakings, tweetings, smells of things overheating – fuses continually blowing as some spectacular short, sparking in purple and green showers, plunged the house in darkness and bad language. Hot soldering irons fizzed in fluxes, many a chassis plugged with warm glowing bottle-valves spread like trays of scones fresh from the oven. One famous time his bedroom curtains accidentally caught fire. Madeleine was as much amazed to see the flaming strands fluttering down past the scullery window as she was by his presence of mind in throwing them out. That had been no bad thing in the circumstances as, along with a number of other combustible ex-army substances his father had acquired, the cupboard outside his bedroom contained several jam jars of gunpowder.

Not much of this bothered Robin, lost in his own world in The Parlour next door. The smell of tables scorched by soldering irons would bleed into Charlotte Brontë's tea party, or, as the unintelligible twang of local police registering on

Peter's ex-army surplus Rll32A scarified the air like circular saws, the revolutionary mob stormed the Royal Apartments calling for vengeance; though John Keats might be dying poetically in wintry Rome, his 'ceasing upon the midnight with no pain' was usually amidst a lot of 'noises off'.

Whatever Peter's pursuits, whether mechanisms, motors or The Goon Show, they tended to involve high outputs of volume, including a short-lived craze for running and servicing a motorbike, accompanied by a roundelay of spanners dropped on concrete and exhausted bursts of fumes.

> Accelerate!
>   A speck, accelerate;
>   A droning dot,
>   A push of dust,
>   A coming cloud
> Accelerate!
>   Becomes a spot,
>   Becomes a mass,
>   A form,
> Accelerate, accelerate,
>   A flashing-by:
> Suddenness of unbreaked breath,
>   Mass again,
>   Then spot
> And dot.

Not least resounded his addiction to Bach's organ music through amplifiers he had built for effect. The upstairs would resonate like a cathedral, the window sashes rattling unless wedged by bits of cardboard. Downstairs Maurice's sing-along-a-Verdi and screaming Wagnerian heroines would require one of them to be turned down in order to preserve Madeleine's sanity caught somewhere in the middle of the sandwich. The lull would reveal Marion's intimidated Dansette record player valiantly attempting to restore some regular rhythm with sound-tracks from the latest musicals. Almost submerged in this musical maze, Robin's own tastes were attempting to form. They centred round a wind-up gramophone and piles of his father's redundant 78s. Nothing at that time thrilled him so much as Caruso's acoustic histrionics in 'Your tiny hand is frozen' from *La Bohème* through the hiss and crackle of surface noise; nor the eight thick black discs with which any weight-lifter would be pleased to practise, bearing Schubert's *Unfinished Symphony,* whetting his appetite for the Romantic repertoire waiting to enslave him.

★ ★ ★ ★ ★

In 1958, Madeleine decided that he was not developing as he should physically, no doubt irritated by his constant procession of sore throats and chills. His indispositions required her to run up and down stairs with trays of steaming food at a rate which would have worn out a missionary. With a sweeping gesture one day she decreed that he must have his tonsils and adenoids out and be done with it. He was shipped off to the Victoria Nursing Home by the fountain in Westbourne Avenue at which Marion had nursed before expanding into social work. From his small room over the front door he commanded an overhead view of the herons keeping a watchful eye on the mermaids. From all of half-a-mile away Peter wrote to him as, languishing on his couch of pain, he subsisted on red jelly and ice-cream:

My Dear Chippendale Chair,

I suppose you are sitting up in your Sheraton bed staring at your tonsils in an Adam jam jar on the Louis XIV table covered with a French tapestry of fabulous value. Not to mention the Chippendale chair in the corner and all the nurses dressed in beautiful crinolines. Taking your medicine in a gold plated teaspoon, looking out of the casement window at the Corinthian orders on top of the front entrance which leads out into the street where all the horse-less carriages rumble by in clouds of smoke.

Doctor Dearn rang us up this morning on the pedestal telephone to tell us all you had got on very well which was a great relief to us all as we had been worrying about you naturally, as Chippendale chairs are of very great value and we don't want any surgeon to damage our prize specimen, which in the very worst junk shop would fetch quite a high price; but you are the best judge of that as I don't really know anything about junk Chippendale chairs as I don't own one yet, not that I really want to. But if someone gave me one I would probably give it to you as I prefer something more comfortable to sit on, which I don't mind really as you are such a dignified authority on old furniture but don't let that go to your head as I'm sure it would do some damage if one hit you on the head as I'm sure they're quite heavy. Just imagine the craftsman himself fashioning a chair from the bare wood in bygone ages, when they really made things, not just knocked them together like today . . .

And so it went on for two large pages barely pausing for breath, one of the most exuberant, bond-forming communications one brother could make with another, humorously encapsulating the essential truth of a singular 14-year-old reinforced in his singularity by the sheer force of presence the Avenues seemed to have on his personality and 25 in particular.

Much to family incredulity, including his own, he had passed the entrance exam to the Junior High School for Art and Crafts in 1956, graduating from Bricknell Avenue Junior School. The High School for Art was an adjunct to the Regional College of Art on Anlaby Road. Though it was strongly biased towards art development, it dealt with general subjects also but with no provision for taking G.C.E.s at the end of the three years, something of a worry to his father. He had, however, been able for the first time to take his hat off to him.

The High School occupied the upper floor of the old Girls' Industrial School beyond the fountain in Park Avenue, dating from 1888. The ground floor housed a school for physically handicapped children and was guarded

A picture of content.

by two emphatic yew trees at the entrance. He became extremely fond of this building with its lengthy red brick frontage, cupola, Dutch gables and twinned lengths of sash windows glinting with white glazing bars like jam squares at school lunch. It entailed short cycle rides from garden to playground, making it seem strange that home life and school life could co-exist under the same protective canopy of trees. He also felt a sense of status in wearing a uniform – the first he had done. The black and terracotta seemed to him less of a symbol of imprisonment than an advertisement of his having actually arrived somewhere in his life. Marion encouraged him to join St. Ninian's Scout Troop at the end of Victoria Avenue: 'good character-building stuff.' He stayed long enough to achieve his first-class badge. He joined the choir of St. Cuthbert's church in Marlborough Avenue; he took drama lessons in Miss Margaret Burnett's tottering studio in the attics of a Georgian terrace house in George Street as he competed in the annual Hull Musical Festival winning book tokens right and left. Only his schoolwork continued to be as scratchy as a threadbare carpet; bread and butter learning seemed to have no relevance to his life as he saw it. He did stagger everyone by coming top in history some terms, but even English, art and music were not easily absorbed and developed. There seemed to be too much of everything to do. His reports would say 'he works only at what interests him – a good machine wasted'. He sometimes wondered if his teachers were working at what interested them; he often got the impression they were not.

On leaving the High School for Art his father, still 'seriously worried' about his academic record, arranged through his network of contacts, for him to join the G.C.E. year at Wilberforce High School in Margaret Street. He was abjured to 'work like stink' at his five chosen subjects: English language and literature, history, art and music. It was a large undertaking for a year but fortunately the surroundings were sympathetic. The building, once Hull

Grammar School, was another of those familiar Victorian piles contemporary with the Avenues. It lay at the end of another leafy ride through Pearson Park absorbing the atmosphere as a matter of right with no thought of tomorrow.

Tomorrow involved knowing what one wished to do with one's life having left school. Of one thing he was certain – he had no burning desire to go into the bank. This was an easy let-out as there was no way he would have been let in. He wanted to paint pictures, write books, be a concert pianist, a poet like Philip Larkin and a famous actor – all at once. The latter lasted only until his father told him he would have to go away to drama school then join a repertory company which would mean having to live on a shoe string in dingy lodgings with no home comforts and definitely no Parlour.

'Like my early days in the bank,' he said, 'you will spend a lot of time making tea, sweeping floors and getting nowhere fast.' He also had set ideas about the lack of morals he considered rampant in professional theatre circles, worried about their corruptive potential on his sheltered son.

By 1960, life not rooted in the Avenues seemed as inconceivable to Robin as a year without Christmas. But as he began to mature he was noticing subtle changes in his environment. The empty straight vistas were becoming spotted with parked vehicles as more residents invested in private transport, using the buildings in the ten-foots as garages. Maurice had been given a car in the mid '50s, a maroon 1938 spoke-wheeled Morris 8 with ribbed leather seats and indicators which always jammed, needing a hefty thump behind them to flip them up out of the car's sides. This mobile biscuit tin had been lovingly christened 'Faith' as it was the main ingredient, after petrol, needed to make her work. But all the faith in the world, however powerful, was not strong enough to get her to the top of a steep hill without most of her occupants having to get out first.

Peter's enthusiasm for motors led him to follow his motorbike with a scarlet convertible which burst into flames one day. It was followed by a nippy two-tone green vintage convertible on which he lavished much care and attention. Marion took over Faith when Maurice bought a black Daimler which wallowed round corners at the mercy of his indifferent gear-changing.

A petrol bus service had been introduced down Park Avenue making Robin wonder if it was responsible for so many ill-fitting windows, crooked lintels and leaning houses. Back in November of 1955, prior to the road being re-laid to accommodate the buses, the City Engineer's Department had reported on a survey of properties along the route. Number 25 was considered to be in generally sound condition but riddled with fine cracks and crazings at all angles. The porch keystone had dropped half an inch, the downstairs bay window sill had moved quarter of an inch with the concrete round it settling over an inch – problems soon identified and rectified. He regarded many of these structural blemishes with affection, for, though the house was full of solid distinctive furniture, the rooms were decorated plainly so it was easy to see additional features: a spray of cracks on the scullery ceiling exactly composing a smiling mask. These familiar signs of ageing were a natural part of the environment, like wrinkles on a well-loved face.

Outside the Avenues' rarefied boundaries the starker realities of human existence spilled out of newspapers and wireless sets: the testing in 1953 and 4 of Russian and American H-bombs, the mushroom cloud becoming a sinister symbol of doom for mankind; the wave of 1955 sightings of supposed flying saucers; the Suez crisis of 1956; the British H-bomb testing at Christmas Island in 1957; the Campaign for Nuclear Disarmament's first Aldermaston march in 1958 and in 1959, a Russian space probe's photographs of the far side of a moon which shone on the first section of Britain's M1 motorway to open.

Not since Nanny's stroke had external forces governed the direction of the future at 25. But now, at this critical point in Robin's development, fate edged in with its paring knife. After a 30-year banking career in Hull, Maurice was offered and accepted promotion to the managership of the St. Nicholas Street branch of the Midland Bank in Scarborough. This would be for the last five years before his retirement; he had indeed counted himself fortunate to have remained established in one place for so long when many of his colleagues were fated to be shovelled from this town to that. It had been fortuitous that Hull contained enough branches for him to work his way through.

Robin understood that his father would find it too much to drive to Scarborough and back five days a week and that residence on the spot was the only option. This whole concept of change was something he, as a late developer, was emotionally unprepared for and ill-equipped to deal with.

VI
LAND OF LOST CONTENT

Into my heart an air that kills
From yon far country blows:
What are those blue remembered hills,
What spires, what farms are those?

That is the land of lost content,
I see it shining plain,
The happy highways where I went
And cannot come again.

A.E. Housman
A Shropshire Lad

It seemed incredible then that improving technology could spread world news so swiftly and that here was the potential for instant knowledge of other things, other places, other peoples. In everyday life, however, self-knowledge is somewhat slower and harder to achieve. In the months preceding the inevitable move Robin realised, with a discomfort that fumed his consciousness like burnt feathers, that it was set to disperse the family unit from its identifying anchor. His father had arranged for him to attend the Scarborough School of Art that September in order to study for the National Diploma in Design, a qualification of some standing he felt would do his son good. There was talk of converting 25 into flats for Marion and Peter, who were to remain with their careers in Hull, but it proved unfeasible; Marion had recently become engaged to Statuesque Stuart so for the year before her marriage, she and Peter took on a flat at 14, Victoria Avenue.

'Even today,' said Robin, 'it is still a mystery to me why I didn't insist on remaining behind also and doing my Diploma at the Hull College. I think my parents felt that I wasn't mature enough to survive on my own which was probably true. They would have worried and then so should I. But it would have been grand to have a go, nevertheless. How could I know what an effect the move would have on me – how I would have liked the force of destiny to be on my terms – in my time – so I could pace myself? I almost felt I was going for an intermediate break and that I'd soon be back where I belonged. For that reason it never occurred to me to say farewell to Jamie, so sure was I we'd soon pick up where we left off.

'I can't believe how undemonstratively I allowed some grey and gloomy agent in a fusty jacket to invade our family fabric, stick his nose into private cupboards and corners, poke his officialdom into The Parlour and mumble, 'That fireplace isn't real,' trespass in the garden and, with total ignorance of the house's significance in our lives, grudgingly suggest that it might, with luck, fetch £2,500 on a good day.

'I am still amazed at how nebulously I submitted to the stranglehold of the inevitable – how I stood by while potential owners invaded The Parlour and gave amused shudders at what it had taken half my lifetime and most of my personality to create. To subject it to such treatment seemed cruel and ungrateful after all the protection, warmth and joy it had given me – small thanks indeed for making me, to a large extent, what I am.

'Nor did our exodus leave the house to some degree of serenity as the eventual new owner, a mean little man with a mouth as tight as a rusty letterbox, kept arriving and disarriving with his own things as we were trying to empty it of ours. His constant chivvying to be quick, his sneery instructions not to lean things against walls in case they marked them, to make sure we didn't dirty those carpets he'd bought from us, did as much psychological damage as the blitz of 20 years ago would have done physically. Now *I* was the refugee and this person had got the better bargain.

'The peace of the garden embraced me as I said farewell, realising what a luxury permanence must be; but I had hardly stood on the empty Parlour floorboards for the last time before the sordid individual was elbowing me out with a tut-tut and tearing my fireplace to bits, streaking jagged wounds across my wallpaper. I would have found some small contentment had I known I was entrusting my heritage to someone I and the family at least liked.

'Marion and Peter were to stay behind a little longer to settle the remaining items in Victoria Avenue and, as I discovered later, to argue vociferously with our insensitive successor. My parents and I gathered in the hall to say temporary goodbyes to them as we had to be in Scarborough before the van. Marion, sitting at the top of the stairs sobbing her heart out, refused to come down; Peter, crying with a stiff upper lip, escorted us to the car, by this time a great grey-silver Humber I had christened The Vomit Box. In a daze I wandered down the garden path and picked a handful of golden rod I've kept pressed to this day.

'As I slumped on the back seat I put it safely in the bag I carried. Through the paper I felt the wooden object's reassuring presence and peeped just once inside. I was comforted by the words DEXTER'S KEY WEST COLORADO MADURO. I had found it empty of its chandelier pieces swept with a pile of rubbish in a corner of the study. Much to my father's bemusement I retrieved it without a word – we were each other's secrets once more.

'I hope I didn't let myself go without a backward glance but I have a sneaking suspicion I might have. I had never seen my brother upset

Golden Rod from 25.

before and it touched me deeply. I wanted to hold him and be held by him; but not through my doing I was being whisked round Beverley Road corner in fourth gear feeling like a pet snatched from his owner. I wanted the musty smell of the study; the glinting warmth of The Parlour as I wrote poetry; the rustling shade of the silver birch whispering over my easel as I painted; the assuring bell from the Convent signifying the indissoluble permanence of the Angelus. The atmosphere of all these remained to be soaked up, but like a leaking tap was now draining to waste because I could not be there to save it in a crystal cup.'

> I dreamed last night
> And woke up tense and couched in care;
>   A door to a road had opened
> And I stood naked on an empty stair.
>
> Though I have been some time away
> It might be only yesterday
>   I left my home. Memory's flight
> Is stronger in the empty night:
>   The removal van has exiled my world –
>   Windows are stripped, floors are bare;
>   The door to the road is open
> And I stand on the empty stair.
>
> I lived my dream again last night
> And woke up calling to the air;
>   The door to the world is open wide
>   But I stand vulnerable –
> Alone on the empty stair.

★ ★ ★ ★ ★

In his parent's more modern house he had naturally created a Parlour but it seemed a poor imitation of the real thing – a pastiche without a soul. The light and air were wrong – there was no tradition of personal identity in its fabric, however many hideous vases and cracked old pots tried to rekindle its spirit. His father's study, too, had been re-established, but it was devoid of much that had given it soul and mystery over the accumulation of years; moves have a habit of thinning out life, and Maurice had been as much a collector in his own way as his son.

The first opportunity he had of revisiting Hull was in the Christmas holiday. He stayed with Marion and Peter in Victoria Avenue and visited Gough and Davy's to buy a bust and long-playing record of Liszt's Piano Concertos to boost his collection now ousting 78s. Though he had come to terms in his own way with the loss of 25, there was no way his steps could be prevented from its threshold. Outwardly the house was as he remembered, which made it more difficult to accept as someone else's. Had it not been for the thought of the horrid little man the other side of the green front door, he would have attacked the knocker in a polite but proprietorial manner asking to see round.

Every time he came back over the next two years he felt compelled to keep an eye on the place. Its appearance never changed – the lilac and golden rod still bloomed; the announcing knocker waited on the front door; the dark windows kept their own counsel. But he noticed a change in the Avenues. They seemed less reposeful. He saw how the through-traffic had increased along with parked vehicles; one had to go about more cautiously as a current article in the *Hull Daily Mail* testified with the headline, NOSE TO TAIL IN THE AVENUES. The reporter noted that Park Avenue was considered worst by its residents, with traffic reduced to single file by rows of up to 15 cars parked on either side. He also said that when he drove along to see for himself, weaving round them was rather like being in a slalom race at the Winter Olympics. Residents, too, were complaining of noise nuisance, road hazards, radio and television interference and the unsightliness of it all. He added, rather tartly, that complaints came from those residents without cars. When they owned them they stopped complaining. 'But,' as he said, 'if you move them on, where can they go?'

The pavements' square flagstones, however, had gone, replaced with runways of grey tarmac; the gas standards had gone, replaced with thin nebulous pipes curved over like long-necked monsters without bodies, their brainless heads spilling depressive orange light.

The successful completion of the Intermediate stage of his Diploma gave him the excuse to leave Scarborough by choosing Exhibition Design for his final two years which the Hull College provided but the Scarborough College did not. It was the nearest he could get to stage design and the creating of environments. But his parents took his choice with a pinch of salt, knowing that the true reason was his difficulty in settling out of Hull. They wisely left him to find his own lodgings which could not be with his sister and brother – Marion was now married and living opposite Pickering Park; Peter had gone to Manchester University to study for a post-graduate degree in electronics. The important issue was to obtain lodgings in or near the Avenues, not an easy task when one is not sure how to go about it. He was wandering about the Avenues one day soaking up the atmosphere and lingering opposite 25 like a child shut out from a party. After a while a lady of about 40 with fair hair emerged and crossed over to him.

'I'm sorry,' he faltered with his most winning smile, hoping to forestall possible indignation. 'I didn't mean to be nosey.'

'Well, you have been here rather a long time,' she replied nicely.

'It's only that I used to live at 25 and like coming back to look at it. I rather miss it, I'm afraid.'

'Well, come in and have a look round, then,' she said unexpectedly. Completely disarmed he followed her across the road and up the well known path already, in those strides more his than hers. It transpired that she had bought it from the original purchaser a year previously but had not altered it in any way. Robin hardly dare believe that he would see the study fireplace again, look through The Parlour window and stand under the silver birch's shimmering clusters.

As Mrs. Eyre took him from room to room, his reason began petrifying into affronted anger. The squalid little man may not have stayed long but it had obviously given him enough time to strip the place of much of its character. Gone were all the fireplaces and chimneypieces upstairs; downstairs, repellent porridge-tiled excrescences insulted the chimney breasts. The stained-glass bay-window with French doors had been replaced by an inappropriate metal-framed rectangle too small and too high. Picture rails had been removed; the window seat in Peter's bedroom had gone. The Parlour looked like a store room and the scullery-kitchen and veranda were stark with strip lights and cheap yellow paint.

Nor were these broadsides restricted to the interior. The unimpeachable silver birch remained, but instead of a graceful Roman candle of fluttering foliage, only a truncated stump creaked about eight-feet into the air like a vandalised monument. Many trees and shrubs had been removed altogether and the sandpit, site of The Shack, had sunk along with the general contour of the garden to a grassy depression. Yet, for all the carnage, he felt the spirit of the place reach out to him and catch at his emotional hooks. All he could say was, 'It wasn't like this in my day.' Mrs. Eyre thoughtfully left him to his feelings, calling him in shortly for a cup of tea and a chat – a somewhat one-sided business leaving her in no doubt as to the significance of 25 and the Avenues in his life. When he told her he was returning to Hull to study she asked him whether he had anywhere to live.

'If you wish,' she said, 'you could come here.'

Robin thought he must have misheard her. Amused by his incredulity, she told him that she was on the University's books for female student accommodation but as she liked him did not see why she could not stretch a point in his case, as long as everyone agreed. This she would find out when the girls returned in a week for the new term. She was willing to let him have The Parlour back to decorate and furnish as he wished. Money and a commencing date could be discussed later. He gave her his contact address and she promised to confirm arrangements as soon as she was able.

'I can't describe what I felt as I left,' he said. 'My whole life seemed to unfocus then focus again. Nothing else mattered. I was about to drop back into my mould. What a piece of luck. How should I treat The Parlour? All its furniture would be returned to its proper place so I could put back the Regency stripe in a faithful reconstruction of one of my favourite schemes. Or should it be a fetching little number in Tudorbethan panelling done properly this time in cardboard? But I'd love to have a go at creating the snug of an old English coaching inn of the 1820s, heavy with churchwarden pipes, lanterns and *papier-mâché* food. Concerns about how to build a generous ingle-nook fireplace completely ousted more mundane considerations as to how it was going to feel to be living in my house which was not my house crowded with people who were not my family.

'A week later, good at her word, Mrs Eyre rang me. She was full of apologies. She had had an unfortunate row with one of her students who had now threatened to inform the University that a dreaded male was to live in their midst. As the establishment was designated as being for females only, the breach of contract would result in its termination. I was, however, welcome to call in any time.

'Let down as I felt by circumstance, I began to see that it might have been a blessing in disguise. The arrangement would have been a fragile image of what it once was with none of the freedoms nor permanency. If nothing else it had brought home to me the virtual impossibility of reharnessing the past other than in the mind, which can be wonderfully selective. There 25 would remain unchanged inside and out representing enduring security. Life's realities need tempering with fantasy in order to keep them in proportion.

'In the meantime the reality of where to live was soon provided by my sister's generous offer of accommodation. At least I was back under the high-piled skies of the East Riding – that reality pleased me very much – and on my own terms too, though the design course turned out to have been the wrong choice, the arid opposite of my natural talents. Unable to cope with the technicalities of scale drawings and constant mathematical snares, I figured out that my only option was to return to the North Riding and complete my Diploma in painting and ceramics, which I should have stayed with in the first place. Father had been irritatingly right as usual: 'See what comes of letting your heart rule your head!'

His parents were happy in Scarborough and remained there after Maurice retired. But once Robin successfully gained his Diploma he felt free to return to Hull. Instead of using his new qualification in a professional capacity he chose to work for an antique dealer on Spring Bank and live in the Avenues. On a wage of £6 a week he paid £5 for a delightful attic room overlooking the gardens at The Hollies Private Hotel at 96, Park Avenue. Here he wrote a short story, *The Wounded Phoenix,* about two brothers who bought back their old home and restored it to live in. He also embarked on his first piece of sustained writing, a novel in the third person called *The Nanny-Goat Kids* based on his experiences of school bullying.

A chance meeting with the Goodman family, now moved to 16, Park Avenue, led to their offer of accommodation. With the two elder children away at University and the two youngest, Roy and Malcolm, still at home, it was good to be with a family of busy youth as he had been at 25, with music as a stimulating life-force. He even rejoined St. Cuthbert's church choir which Roy, though still a schoolboy, was directing from the organ. Mrs. Eyre had moved from 25, which was taken on, along with other Avenues properties, as a residence for nuns and children of the Sisters of Charity of St. Vincent de Paul in Queen's Road. Great wooden divisions were visible running into the bay-windowed rooms at right angles so that each compartment was lit by half a window.

The Hoggarts and Jouberts had left Hull; most of the original neighbours had moved or died – there were no more toffees from Mrs. Charter's tin. Mrs. Kirkby and Miss Bayston on Princes Avenue had retired; the Brigand's was now an Indian takeaway; the Avenues, increasingly popular for student flats, were imperceptibly losing their muffled exclusivity under an influx of restless traffic and noise. Epidemics of 'home improvement' and D.I.Y., one of the less attractive features of the 1960s, produced many an ill-considered blemish with which to torment a unified length of architecture. His cycle rides round Hull's old haunts revealed a city which, in the light of his maturing outlook, now seemed to be in the grip of an imbalance between development and depression. Jamie, too, was gone.

1967 terminated this last phase of Avenueitis as his parents worried about his life meandering as aimlessly as a crack in one of his pots. His father organised for him to join the design and display department of a notable Scarborough retail store at £8 a week which he hoped would help him 'settle down'. Reluctant as he was to place further strain on his mother's nerves, he complied. But it seemed ironical that for the third time he was so easily back in the place he least wanted to be. For a while, though, he had been in charge, touching base with his roots. Fundamental as the Avenues would always be to him, he had come some way at last to finding out how to let the head do a little ruling of the heart.

★ ★ ★ ★ ★

'That wasn't quite the end, though,' he said, pausing reflectively. 'Just when I thought I had bravely consigned the Avenues and 25 to the lumber rooms of nostalgia they inveigled me once again, some 20 years later, as much as to say, 'You can't clear us out of your life as easily as that.' Let me explain.

'During those intervening years I progressed from department store to Teachers' Training College in Scarborough as a mature student. Then came 15 years teaching art and ceramics in Yorkshire and, after my marriage, in Sussex. Peter had married the year before me and settled in Hull. As we sat together in church awaiting the entrance of his bride, Val, I thanked him, before his commitment to her, for being such a loyal friend and brother to me over the years – and a patient one. I had to say what I felt at that moment though he looked a little abashed. As Wagner's *Bridal March* began its organic declamation and we joined the congregation's rising shuffle, I felt him gently squeeze my arm.

'Thank you, dear boy,' he said. 'You're a good lad really.'

'My parents then returned to the Hull area to be near the family during my mother's final illness, an affliction of the nervous system. She died in 1977 aged 70 but my father lived on another 11 years, dying aged 83 on 6 July, 1988, my birthday. It was an undemonstrative death, like his personality, whilst enjoying coffee with friends at the Pearson Park Hotel, an apt locality in which to release his soul.

'His passing allowed my artistic but more level-headed wife, Rose, and me to fulfil our increasing ambition of living in France. Here was the long-postponed opportunity to regulate our lives on our terms, at the same time putting to good use our experiences as teachers. We bought and restored a period farmhouse near Bordeaux. where we ran painting holidays for relaxed people, providing full board and smiling tuition.

'On 9 March, 1990, Peter came to stay, not because he wanted tuition but more because he felt he needed to be with us for a while. He looked tired, I thought, and admitted he hadn't been sleeping well due to things on his mind. True to his nature, though, he was reluctant to have any fuss made of it. He'd always tended to be secretive about health issues and one knew better than to press him on such matters. He brought me my early birthday present: a recently published book, *An Illustrated History of the Avenues and Pearson Park, Hull.* Amongst the placid sun-bound swathes of Dordogne this package unexpectedly liberated that nostalgia in me I thought I had designated to the proper proportion in my life. I was cheered to learn of the Residents' Association formed in 1970 and the designation of the Avenues as a conservation area four years later. As I read of the strong community spirit in the neighbourhood, the concern for preserving the area's character, its trees and wild life, its distinctive architecture and abundant gardens, 30 years fell away like old plaster revealing how vulnerable the underlying structure of my being still was. With wood smoke scenting the sweet air, many were the suppers with Peter before log fires, the candlelight through many a decanter of Bergerac casting red spears across the white tablecloth. We talked of family life at 25 and of our parents. But, though only 53 he said he felt age taking him over, his phrase being, 'It's *anno domini,* dear boy', at which with characteristic stubbornness he ignored my reprimand for thinking in such a way.

'At 1.40pm on the 16th, I saw him off on his flight home from Bordeaux airport. I was overwhelmed with an unaccountable sadness and involuntarily gave him a huge hug, telling him to look after himself.

'The 'phone rang at 9pm on 7 May, a Bank Holiday in England. It was Marion. She told me that Peter had collapsed and died that morning.

'You shall be spared the anguish as I know, like me, you have imagination. I can tell you, however, that I was too demolished to travel to his funeral four days later, family understanding persuading me that it was not out of order to be absent. On the day, Rose and I purchased a five-foot silver birch from Madame Beauvier's nursery and planted it beside the little vineyard we had, a site of which Peter would have approved, and where only a few short weeks earlier he had rhapsodised over our surroundings and quality of life. It then seemed to me poetic justice to make a donation to the Avenues Residents' Association in memory of his having been born there; it gave me pleasure to think it would be used in connection with a cause so close to my heart.

'My wish has been granted that Peter's tree should thrive as sturdily as the one at 25 it emulated. Twelve years on it surges 30 feet into the Dordognian sky, anthemed each returning spring by golden oriole and nightingales.

INTERLUDE

When, as with my elder brother, the moment comes
    For me to feel at last
That unrelenting stab of mortal pain,
Then slip immortal Mozart on the hi-fi for me,
    Turn up the gain
And face me to the window, though I hear and see
    Nought but numbing vapours closing round my brain.
Though my time to frolic and fade congeal
    And all genius, man and nature assail me in vain,
I would be glad to know I have it thus
And ease me from myself without complaint.

Yet don't stop the blue haze pilfering the purple plain,
Nor airborne stir and clamour of feathered wings
    Above the vale;
Neither bank the sunlight in a vault,
    Or stamp the dance of sound
From golden oriole and nightingale;
Chide not brisk summer zephyrs through the dappled copse
    Dropped with star of Bethlehem, yellow archangel
        And ox-eye daisies round;
Frown never on spotted acres of poppy-flopped corn;
    On silver birch and side-swept poplars
        Fanning out the sky.
Let the smashing thunder vandalise magenta clouds;
Exultant rainbows arc the hurried baling wain
    From crock to crock of gold, far across a yawn
Of polished fields where I shall not exult again.

Do not charge it as my fault
That I reaped these glories as my own;
But rather that my senses
    Made me selfish and bemoan
They can't outlive my heart – that I can go
    In knowledge of their power being done.
        Ah, no! Haze and zephyr and nightingale endure
    So put me to the wall and turn the hi-fi low:
        'Does he now shake his brother's hand and Mozart's
In immortal sun?'

VII

LOOK FORWARD TO YESTERDAY

25 remains the bastion of my soul, the part
　　Which well I heed and made
　　Most polished jewel
In my diadem of life:
　　No mere materials of the builder's trade
But more the footings of my stand on earth
　　Made fast and deeply laid,
True to the plumb line of my heart.

It will not let me go,
　　This keeper of my complex self,
Nor relinquish its familiar hold
　　Upon my willing being.
I am a prisoner of my past
　　And presently content to know
　　That when I'm at my last,
　　It shall receive
My fading hold on sound and seeing.

As these pages testify, orthodox is not a word appropriate to Robin's life. He is the first to agree that it has never been short of the unexpected. As other family problems accompanied his brother's death, he and Rose reached the conclusion that they needed to be back in Yorkshire in order to be on hand in a supporting capacity, particularly to their sister-in-law Val and her two teenage children, Juliet and James. The farmhouse and its two acres was sold and a nearby property more suitable to being left for long periods was bought into from 1992 onwards.

The priority was to find somewhere to live, making the initial choice of the Avenues a logical one. Number 25 was not on the market. Would it have been considered if so? The inevitable compulsion to view might have been enough proof that only in the mind can one return to the land of lost content – that the progress of free, independent spirits is not achieved by reverting to an actual environment so prescriptive in its past associations. It makes the land of found content difficult to discover. 23 had recently sold for £89,000 and 27 for £87,000. The dilapidation of the Gilbert Scott houses near the fountains was a phenomenon which could almost be described as inspired neglect – one had lost half its front, a sorry mess of rubble revealing its drooping skeleton and peeling bowels; one was uninhabitable and one was a burned-out shell. Cheering, though, was the sympathetic replacement of one of Princes Avenue's original terraces incorporating architectural features from its surroundings including sculpted gargoyles on the window keystones.

Apart from 25's change of colour scheme from dark green to white woodwork with a scarlet front door, it remained recognisable despite the absence of golden rod and lilac. Not so 27, its sagging bays propped up on a pair of giant wooden crutches like some Masonic paraplegic. Another pair lent support to 29. Subsidence, encouraged by several dry summers, had not been kind to Hull's clay foundations. Underpinning and rebuilding were required in several areas, a major concern as Robin and Rose viewed a number of properties in Westbourne Avenue, one of which backed onto 25 and had belonged to Mrs. Bottom. It was a curious sensation to peer over the renewed fence and see a space so crucial to formative years from the reverse position, like looking the wrong way through a telescope. It took a great deal of imagination to re-create the significance of that space, spreading there like a poor spectre of past powers. Beethoven's old home at Miss Drasdo's next door was broken up into flats.

The potential customers, though finding the house and garden hugely attractive and tempted not least by the boundary's still guardian poplars, stalled at the degree of slipment. They were alarmed at how much fist could be inserted into the gap between the staircase and the wall to which it was supposed to be attached. Aware of the area's problems and their limited finances, they reluctantly settled for the sounder foundations of a converted Methodist chapel near Beverley. Robin's head had truly ruled his heart this time.

With Park Avenue now providing him with an easy and welcome short cut into town, he could monitor the relay of advancing scaffolding and mountainous skips; many a trodden and rutted grass verge spoke of heavy machinery and forceful labour; the constant spill of banging, drilling and whistling from behind half-reconstructed facades told of continuous rescue. The lines of dwellings were reminiscent of hospital patients awaiting treatment, with Robin, like a relative of Florence Nightingale, traversing the wards to speculate on which patient might be next for surgery. How long before the epidemic spread to 25?

By the Easter of 1994 he found a cavern where his parents' bedroom had been, with a crash of men busily demolishing down into his father's study. Had he beheld this 30 years previously the neighbourhood might well have rung with hysteria; but now he felt only positive relief and gratitude – and a certain surprise at his accumulated objectivity, convincing him of the old adage that perhaps travel does broaden the mind after all.

His attention was equally arrested by a family of ducks who obviously believed in the same philosophy. Having risked beak and wing, they had survived the hazardous expedition from Pearson Park in order to snuggle down contentedly on seemingly preferable pastures contained by an adjacent verge, not a brick's-throw from the mayhem up the garden path.

25 undergoes surgery.

The 1990s continued to be unsettled times for the Avenues with the chunky mature trees, 120 years old and thrusting 60-foot in height, giving rise for concern. Constant pollarding had made some of them prone to rot and decay. A sympathetic replacement programme was already underway with the intention of felling some 20 trees a year over a 30-year period, replacing them with 12-foot saplings of Indian horse chestnut, hybrid lime and Norwegian maple. But this paced approach received a cutting blow when a resident opposite 25 made a successful claim against Humberside Council who owned the trees for their negligence in effectively pruning the limes outside her by now collapsing property. In the heat of subsequent compensation claims it was decided to escalate the programme. But the loss of nearly 100 of the 700 trees in one operation would unavoidably have visual repercussions until the saplings had grown to scale. The section round 25 proved to be one of the most affected, but at least the residents had the dubious comfort of knowing that they were not alone in their distress as similar problems in Anlaby Park and Garden Village required similar action.

A future for the past?
7 Salisbury Street moulders away.

The past with a future.
7 Salisbury Street reborn.

By November, 1995, the two distressed and derelict Gilbert Scott houses were absorbing an £800,000 renovation and rebuilding operation, with the burnt-out shell of 109, Park Avenue, being later demolished and reconstructed in facsimile with the advantage of 100 tons of concrete beneath the foundations in an attempt to counter subsidence. These were by now listed.

Nor were the fountains' mermaids to remain ignored amongst all this surrounding drama. At the beginning of November, a 20-year-old motorist overturned his Rover on the Westbourne Avenue island taking with him the mermaid fronting Salisbury Street. At the end of November a second motorist mounted the Park Avenue island in a desire to know the mermaids better. He was followed next day by a third who not only took all four mermaids with him but demolished the entire edifice. A five-year restoration estimated at £200,000 for both fountains came to a successful conclusion in May, 2001, with Park Avenue's replacement hedged by a dense circle of sturdy municipal planting established, one assumes, to deter future over-familiar road users. There may yet be the possibility of replacing the fountains in Victoria and Marlborough Avenues, neither of which contained distracting mermaids.

At roughly the same time the next generation of the family were taking an interest in the Avenues. Peter's son James, now 25, was on the look-out for a property in which to invest, and amongst others in the town considered 158, Park Avenue, one of the high-pitched Gothic-style houses by the fountain. Much as he relished the area and appreciated its significance in his father's and uncle's lives, other considerations dictated that it would be the wrong choice for him. It was only afterwards that one of life's little coincidences dropped into place: that at the time of looking his age corresponded with the house number his father had been born in.

Back in July, 1988, the Park Avenue Neighbourhood Watch was formed being one of the first 10 in Hull. By that time the Residents' Association was 18-years-old since when the last 14 have been ones of steady commitment and progress. It has to monitor the balance between the neighbourhood's strong sense of historical significance and its also being a living area needing to serve a modern community. This has to be done without losing sight of its intrinsic character – one which needs to be respected and protected, making some 20th-century commodities such as stone-cladding, satellite dishes and U.P.V.C. difficult issues to reconcile. Great care is taken to be sympathetic to the natural beauty of the locality by the encouragement of bulb-planting, a concern for bird and wild life, the care of the grass verges and trees; and the keeping of business and pleasure updated in Newsletters encouraging a democratic approach, often in conjunction with interest shown at Local Council level. One of the happiest innovations has been the support for residents annually to open their gardens to an appreciative public. The two Sundays in July bring much welcomed publicity for one of the Avenues' greatest and most personal attributes.

In 1991 a Conservation Officer maintained that the Avenues, as a desirable

These fallen idols will rise again.

residential locality, was benefiting from the ripple effect of a £450m renaissance currently being pumped into creating Hull's new development schemes. She explained that families who might once have moved further out to estates, suburbs and villages were thinking of buying larger houses further in, with the current fashion for Victorian and Edwardian character contributing to the popularity of an area which offered value and style with convenience.

The late 20th and early 21st centuries are in many ways ages of enlightenment, with conservation and heritage issues more pertinent than at any other time. The fragility of life and the earth that supports it are too often taken for granted and abused. Yet there is a comprehensive awareness of the consequences should an imbalance take stranglehold. Just as the front can be restored to 25 with no jarring evidence of so momentous a problem, so humanity has to adapt to change without losing that essential spirit of quintescent identification; and to trust that increased enlightenment over world issues, both human and environmental, will ensure an auspicious future for all the avenues of our existence and pleasure.

★ ★ ★ ★ ★

One final avenue is still to yield its secret – the communal passage in Park Avenue between 25 and 27 leading to their back gardens. Once in the passageway, Robin ran his hand along the familiar exterior brickwork at the back of his father's old study and family sitting room. But instead of obeying his natural impulse to open the six-foot gate on his left to the closed garden, he had to turn right into what had been the garden of the asthmatic headmistress with difficult lessons. But the green verdant space had long since imploded into an explosion of fun-fair sheds and summerhouses, paths winding through artefacts and rain. He reached the garden's extremity and turned to look back along its length to the house and those on either side. He showed no interest in the garden he had paid to see but went to the fence dividing him from the garden on his right. As he peered from under his umbrella through convenient gaps he could see an undulating green depression – a rough grassy desert of expectancy devoid of features and surrounded by inquisitive poplars, chestnuts and sycamores kept at bay by defiant hedges. There was no black shed, no silver birch.

Then he noticed me staring at him from under my identical umbrella, sensing that I was familiar to him. We were the same height and build – exact contemporaries. He seemed to recognise me; it was probably my nose which I'm told is suggestive of my Greek ancestry. Like him I wear my brown hair longish over my ears. As I approached he saw, I hope, my dark but friendly eyes appraising him intently.

'It's Robin, isn't it?' he said, offering me his hand. 'I thought I recognized you. Have you lost something too?'

'In a way I have,' I half laughed, grasping his hand warmly. A drain gurgled in competition to my medium light voice. 'But it was many years ago. I used to live there and also wanted to see what it looked like.'

'There's not much to see,' he said, trying to be helpful. 'Is it as you remember?'

'It's changed much over the years,' I said, shaking my head. 'The house has too by the look of it. I don't know if I have.' He expressed his fondness for the Avenues, even in bad weather, having known them all his life. I agreed by saying that I still considered the house and garden spiritually mine. He registered that he knew what I meant as our feelings were identical.

I pointed to first floor-level. 'You see that window? That used to be my room – The Parlour. At one time my entire world was concentrated behind that glass. It was my window on the world – it was enough for me.'

Simaltaneously we then said, 'Part of that world still remains glazed there. I expect it always will. You either see it or you don't.'

We considered each other's features – features as familiar to us as our own. He said, 'It's strange, isn't it, how worlds expand the older you get but time to explore them gets shorter. I know I've spoken your thoughts but you've often spoken mine, though what does it really matter which of us thinks and which of us speaks? They both come from one mind – one emotion – one individual.

We are one and the same, you and I – the perfect fusion of ego and alter-ego.'

Comprehending the situation, I could only relax in the knowledge of unconditional acceptance.

'Then,' we said with a smile, 'we should make the most of any exploration we can. Where better to begin than in The Land of Lost Content? We'll share it with one another and each be the other's navigator as we understand ourselves completely. The future could give way at any second – the past is secure.'

★ ★ ★ ★ ★

The heart has its reasons
which are quite unknown to
the head.

Blaise Pascal
1623-62

ENVOI

Now chimney-high, the trees
  Of my early days
Reach cowlwards, their leaves
  Over spilling the clay
Of their verge-plot growth undefiled.
From parapet to sill
  To threshold floor
  They fan in waves
Of mobile greens sun-piled,
  Sun-flourished, as before
And during my many years away.

  Honesty-straight,
The Avenues and pavements pass
  Hedged garden squares up-pathed
To lead-bound rainbow-glass front doors
  And window bays wide-plated across
A new generation of reflective cleric,
  Student, poet, don,
In book lined, leaf-soaked, effervescent hush;
  Woodland blackbird, sparrow, thrush
    And dove
Antheming their closed-round, open minds
  On philosophy, religion, intellect,
  Life's meaning,
Love.

Five o'clock and time for tea!
  And for the sun to be,
    As I recall,
  About as tall
  As the poplar tree
Marking our garden wall.
  How small
The sprint of time
  Since first my fragile innocence,
    From those days on,
Began to fall.

And still they grow,
   The trees now,
Ringing each year round
    With sap-swelled contours
      Row by row,
   Telling of space gone by in part.
And yet, some innocent cell of me is found
In communion with the sprites of youth unbound:
Sanctuary for the heart.

Some unquietness of soul
   Is yet appeased in mind
By returning to myself my own truth
   As I stroll
    Enwombed, entombed, enshrined,
Beneath these vaults of unbiased leaves
Whispering my tree-marked plot
Of yielding and unvanquished youth.

FURTHER READING

Boston, L. M., *Memories (including Memory in a House)*. (Colt Books Ltd., Cambridge, 1992).

Elsom, K., (Ed.), *Hull Personalities*, Part 1. (The Avenues' Press, 1990).

Frostick, E., *The Story of Hull and its People* (Hutton Press, 1990).

Horspool, R. D., *The House of Powolny – Life and Death of a Hull Restaurant*. (Highgate, 2000).

Jenkins, A., *The Forties*. (1977).

Ketchell, C., (Ed.) *An Illustrated History of the Avenues and Pearson Park, Hull*. (The Avenues and Pearson Park Residents' Association, 1989).

Lewis, P., *The Fifties*. (1978).

Markham, J., *Streets of Hull – A History of their Names*. (Highgate, 1989).

Rutherford, I., *Hull as it Was*. (Hendon Publishing Co. Ltd., 1982).

Sheppard, M., Rooney, S., Smith, D., (Ed.) *A Short History of the Avenues and Pearson Park Conservation Area*. (James Freeman, 1976).

Severs, D., 18 Folgate Street – *The Tale of a House in Spitalfields*. (Chatto & Windus 2001).

Smith, J., *Hull in the 1950s*. (Hutton Press, 1994) .